DATE DUE

DATE DUE		
DEC 1 0 2001		
DEC 0 5 2002		
DEC 1 5 2003		

NOV 1 1 1995
JAN - 4 1996
DEC 1 4 1998

MAR - 3 2000

JAN 2 4 1996
MAR 2 2

JAN 3 0 1996
NOV

FEB 1 2 1996
JUL 2 7 2001

MAR 2 1 1996
NOV 1 0 2001

The Medicalization of Eating: Social Control in an Eating Disorders Clinic

A VOLUME IN
CONTEMPORARY ETHNOGRAPHIC STUDIES
Editor: Jaber F. Gubrium, *Department of Sociology, University of Florida*

CONTEMPORARY ETHNOGRAPHIC STUDIES

Editor: **Jaber F. Gubrium**
Department of Sociology
University of Florida

Oldtimers and Alzheimer's: The Descriptive Organization of Senility
Jaber F. Gubrium, *Marquette University*

Becoming Doctors: The Professionalization of Medical Students
Jack Hass and William Shaffir, *McMaster University*

The Web of Leadership: The Presidency in Higher Education
William G. Tierney, *Pennsylvania State University*

Hearts and Minds, Water and Fish: The IRA and INLA
in a Northern Irish Ghetto
Jeffrey A. Sluka, *Massey University, New Zealand*

Caring Strangers: The Sociology of Intergenerational Relations
Dale J. Jaffe, *University of Wisconsin, Milwaukee*

A Paradoxical Community: The Emergence of a Social World
Haim Hazan, *Tel-Aviv University*

The Medicalization of Eating: Social Control in an Eating Disorder Clinic
Robin Jane Marie Vogler, *Community Mental Health Services of*
Belmont, Harrison & Monroe Counties, St. Clairsville, Ohio

The Medicalization of Eating: Social Control in an Eating Disorders Clinic

by   **ROBIN JANE MARIE VOGLER**
*Community Mental Health Services
of Belmont, Harrison and Monroe
Counties
St. Clairsville, Ohio*

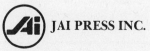 JAI PRESS INC.

Greenwich, Connecticut   *London, England*

Library of Congress Cataloging-in-Publication Data

Vogler, Robin Jane Marie
   The medicalization of eating : social control in an eating
disorders clinic / by Robin Jane Marie Vogler
     p.   cm.
   Includes bibliographical references.
   ISBN 1-55938-524-3
   1. Eating disorders—Treatment—Social aspects. 2. Social
control. I. Title.
   [DNLM:] 1. Eating Disorders—therapy. 2. Health Facilities.
3. Social Control, Informal. 4. Social Control, Formal. WM 175
V884m 1993
616.85′2606—dc20
DNLM/DLC
for Library of Congress   93-12496
                                              CIP

Copyright © 1993 JAI PRESS INC.
55 Old Post Road, No. 2
Greenwich, Connecticut 06836

JAI PRESS LTD.
The Courtyard
28 High Street
Hampton Hill
Middlesex TW 12 1PD
England

ISBN NUMBER 1-55938-524-3

Library of Congress Catalogue Number 00-000

Manufactured in the United States of America

Contents

Acknowledgments

I am very grateful to a number of people for their enthusiasm, support and guidance throughout the research and analysis of this ethnography. This study was originally a dissertation presented to Drs. Carol Warren, Barrie Thorne and Nancy Lutkehaus at the University of Southern California. They gave me their advice, critical evaluation and encouragement. Although confidentiality does not permit me to personally acknowledge them, I want to thank all the staff, patients and members of Overeaters Anonymous who encouraged and supported my work. Thank you for so candidly sharing your lives with me. I wish to thank my friends and family for all their caring and encouragement. Special thanks to Mary and Dan, my in-laws, for their moral support and practical assistance throughout this project. I would also like to thank my friend, Lynn Rippe, who gave unstintingly of her time, wisdom and unfailing optimism. Thank you for laughing good-naturedly while spending long nights at the computer away from your own family. To my husband, Danny, and my son, Dac, I owe the joy and magic in my life.

Chapter I

Introduction

Changes in attitudes and beliefs surrounding the "ideal" size and shape of women in American society have created a plethora of control agents and agencies that label women's appearance and eating behavior as deviant. According to the labeling perspective (Becker 1963; Erickson 1962; Lemert 1951, 1967) it is the societal reaction to the act and not the behavior itself that determines deviance. Thus, if a woman violates a norm governing physical appearance (Schur 1984) she is likely to be labled a deviant, which negatively affects her self conception. She is likely to begin to think of herself as a deviant and to enter into a career that perpetuates this stigmatizing label.

Unlike many other forms of deviancy, appearance and eating behavior are not formally considered criminal behavior under the jurisdiction of the criminal justice system. However, weight and eating have become the focus of the medical and therepeutic community, as clearly demonstrated in the recent proliferation of eating disorder clinics across the United States. Women who enter these clinics as patients do so in order to recover from what is defined by our society as a stigmatizing social problem and a medical illness.

In the "right of passage" or "transition" through a hospital treatment program, patients go through a process similar to the generic sequence defined by Arnold Van Gennep (1960). Van Gennep states that all rights of passage have three phases: separation, margin (or limen), and reaggregation. The separation phase segregates the individual from the profane world.

1

During the second "liminal" phase, individuals are perceived as entities in transition, without the position or status of the past or the future. The final reaggregation (or reincorporation) phase celebrates the individual's return to a stable state. The individual is expected to behave appropriately in accordance with his or her newly acquired position in society.

In a sociological analysis of the moral career of the mental patient, Erving Goffman (1961) identifies three distinct phases which are very similar to Van Gennep's anthropological work on ceremonies of status transition. Goffman identifies these three stages of the hospitalization process as follows: The period prior to hospital entry which he labels the "prepatient" phase; the period in the hospital, he calls the "inpatient" phase; and the period after discharge, he titles the "ex-patient" phase. In addition, he discusses the sequence of changes that occurs both internally, such as the image of self and felt identity; and externally, as in patterns of social control that are exerted by the patient and the staff.

Using Van Gennep's and Goffman's research as a framework, I analyze the moral career of the eating disorder patient as she enters the hospital system, works her program as a liminal entity, and finally is discharged to a new "recovered" status in society.

In addition, I am specifically concerned with the social control processes utilized by the staff in the eating disorders clinic. Staff define an eating disorder as any form of dysfunctional eating that inevitably leads to one of the following illnesses: anorexia nervosa, bulimia, and obesity. My analysis is based on five and a half months of participant observation at a medical facility which included inpatient treatment for an eating disorder. I will refer to this unit as the Section of Eating Disorders (SED).

Staff seek to ensure that patients internalize the normative expectations and standards of behavior of SED (and the larger society) by means of social control. Once patients incorporate within their personalities the standards of behavior required by SED staff, these patients begin to evolve an identity consistent with the unit's philosophy. Thus, social control becomes self-control, and eventually the patient no longer needs to rely on the external controls provided by the staff. Therefore, at discharge, the patients who are perceived as "recovered" are internally monitoring their conduct in accordance with the norms of SED.

There are two major mechanisms of social control operating throughout the hospital career of these patients. The first mechanism is the application of stigmatizing labels. Labels are used to admit patients, and to design and justify the "appropriate" treatment plans for the patients. The second mechanism is emotion management. Staff believe that eating behavior is controlled by patients learning to successfully manage the expression of emotions. Staff use both of these mechanisms to help patients develop new frameworks of social reality and maintain appropriate behaviors. As patients progress from the intake stage, through "getting better," to discharge, each phase is characterized by special variations of the labeling and emotion management practices of social control.

Labeling or typification occurs on both a formal and an informal level. Formally, a patient is admitted to SED and is given a diagnosis of a metal disorder derived from the *Diagnostic and Statistical Manual III* (DSM-III) (APA 1980) in order to receive treatment and insurance reimbursement. Informally, labeling operates at two levels. First, staff typify all patients as "sick" and "compulsive overeaters" with specific problems relating to emotional expression. Second, staff label patients as "good" or "bad" according to the degree to which the patients accept organizational control. Staff expects patients to assume the identity of "compulsive overeaters" and to display minimal resistance to staffs' instructions and the social conventions of the unit. In addition, staff are concerned with the assessment of each patient's unique "potential" for recovery.

At hospital admission, staff begin the process of redefining the patient's identity. Patients are informed they are "insanely sick;" they possess a "progressively lethal disease." All attempts to justify or interpret their eating as a reaction to social factors are systematically neutralized by staff. Now, in order to be accepted by her audience (most patients are females) and proceed toward recovery, the patient must incorporate (or at least display) a medical interpretation of her conduct and the label it generates.

The patient's shifting interpretations of her eating behavior, at admission and during hospitalization, clearly demonstrate that reality is renegotiated and reconstructed within the micro-setting of the SED. Essentially, each patient develops a social career based around her recovering from an eating disorder, and this career permeates her identity in almost every context of her life.

Her identity is tainted because eating disorders are perceived by society as intensely discrediting. Every patient on SED possesses two of the three broad categories of discrediting attributes that Goffman (1963) describes as stigmatizing. All patients demonstrate some form of physical symptomotology related to an eating disorder: excessive thinness for anorexia nervosa (Bruch 1973); destruction of dental enamel in bulimia (House, Grisius, and Bliziotes 1981) and overabundance of adipose tissue mass for obesity (Bray 1979). In addition, all patients have the discrediting character defect of either demonstrating or acknowledging some form of aberrant eating behavior. Patterns commonly reported are: starving in anorexia nervosa (Palazzoli 1967); binge-purging in bulimia (Boskind-White and White 1983); and chronic overeating in obesity (Garn, LaVelle, and Pilkington 1984).

Howard Becker (1963) notes that a deviant status such as an eating disorder is perceived as a "master status" that becomes identified as the person's essential character. Such imputation of a deviant identity is described by Goffman (1963) as a "spoiled identity." Therefore, the patient's character and behavior are re-evaluated on the unit using this new, devaluing identity of "compulsive overeater."

Once the labeling and new identity of the patient are tentatively established, the process of "getting better" (the liminal phase) commences. Many of the properties of liminality on SED correspond to those occurring in tribal rituals reported by Turner (1967, p. 111). These common characteristics include: reduction to the same (powerless) status level, homogeneity, elimination of private property, sexual continence, total obedience to staff and treatment philosophy, equality, "sacred" instruction, and acceptance of suffering. During this phase, the patient is typified as "recovering" or "not recovering" to the extent that she publicly displays an extensive personality transformation.

The basic premise of the transformational process is that once the individual hits her unique "bottom of physical, emotional, and spiritual despair," she commences on a somewhat linear growth pattern toward recovery. In order to demonstrate successful transformation, staff observe the patient "working the program." Working the program consists of various assignments and rituals that promote a patient's awareness of her condition (self-stigmatization); acceptance of assistance from a power greater than herself ("appropriate" dependency); and finally, presumed relief of emotions (such as guilt, resentment, and fear) by actions taken in the form of confession and amends towards others.

The ultimate goal of working the program is for the patient successfully to manage the expression of the emotions that are presumed to control eating behavior. It is not emotions per se that are forbidden on SED. Arlie Hochschild (1983) in her seminal work *The Managed Heart* defines "emotion management" or "emotion work" as the private management of feelings in order to project a public display of emotion which, in turn, produces a desired outcome. She further suggests that culturally specific "feeling rules" designate the emotions it is deemed appropriate to experience, as well as to display, in various kinds of circumstances. Hochschild shows that stewardesses and bill collectors engage in "emotion management"—evoking, shaping, or suppressing feelings of different kinds—in order to avoid committing "affective deviance." Therefore, in this particular organizational setting, proper emotion management is seen as the most effective means of controlling eating behavior.

Mechanisms of social control dealing with emotion management include: staff observation of patient affect and behavior; rituals of reformation; and normalization ceremonies. While observation and rituals are most likely experienced during the getting better stage, normalization ceremonies occur exclusively during the discharge phase of the patient's career.

The patient's response to the mechanisms of control used by the staff is storytelling. Storytelling, in this setting, is the reconstruction of a biography to repudiate a bad, old self and incorporate the rebirth of a new, recovered self. Most often, stories take the form of either tales of the painful past (prior to hospitalization), or stories of being unengaged (those who feel to be or are seen by the staff as marginal patients). The climax of all storytelling events is the final "good-bye" in the form of a luminary saga told during the normalization celebration.

During the discharge phase there are three signs of recovery that determine the extent to which a patient is seen as either "recovered" or "not recovered." These signs are primarily based on the redirection of inner negative feelings that had (in the past) inevitably precipitated a binge or some type of dysfunctional eating behavior. In other words, the patient demonstrates successful emotion management. The signs are physical progress, emotional health, and spiritual development (significantly, not weight loss). In addition, these signs are subjectively measured by staff via the patient's storytelling. Clear demonstration of signs of progress in treatment contribute to the staff's impression that the patient is "recovered." And therefore, a quicker and smoother transition to aftercare status and eventual termination of hospitalization occurs.

At discharge, staff deem a patient as recovered/not recovered from the disease of compulsive overeating. However, this does not mean that staff ascribe a "normal" identity to patients (using the term normal as Goffman [1963] has, to contrast with those who are stigmatized). As Laslett and Warren (1975, p. 79) propose in their analysis of obesity as a type of deviance:

> Individuals may change their behavior and way of life from deviant to normal on some relevant dimension, but may retain stigmatized identity connected with that same dimension.

In other words, a compulsive overeater may recover to the extent that she controls her eating behavior and leads a normal way of life. But according to staff, she will forever carry the stigmatized identity of a compulsive overeater even in the stigma is no longer visibly apparent because her identity will always be discreditable.

This study demonstrates on the micropolitical level the process by which a field of behavior, in this case eating, becomes a field of social and medical intervention. By studying the relationship between the eating disorder patient and various significant others, I analyze the construction and negotiation of reality within one microsetting of our society. One conclusion of this study is that the development of the eating disorder patient's deviant career, and the eventual social control and transformation of these women by means of medical therapeutic intervention, is a result of contemporary ideology concerning weight and also of a new type of capitalistic entrepreneurship within our society.

However, the relationship between eating, appearance, and the social order has not remained constant over time. This contemporary phenomenon that I am addressing has not always been perceived as a medical problem. The following literature review discusses the social construction of eating disorders from various schools of thought, including historical and cross-cultural perspectives.

THE SOCIAL CONSTRUCTION
OF EATING DISORDERS

Initially, fat was a means of survival of the human species. It was not a moral, legal, religious or aesthetic issue, as it appears today (Allon 1976). Food was the economic means of survival due to the high amount of famine that has threatened to end the species throughout human history. Thus the storage of fat in humans was highly efficient for survival. However, weight and eating behavior have become regulated by social arrangements over time. Norms governing personal appearance and eating patterns are associated with social factors, both historically and anthropologically.

One primary connection between food, appearance, and femininity is the female form as a pleasure object. Throughout western history women have attempted to obtain the size dictated as fashionable by the time or the culture. Orbach (1978, 1982) notes that from past to present a man's wage is considered his primary asset; a woman's body is hers.

Women tend to be influenced by the mass media which stress the necessary, but not sufficient, quality of thinness. The media insist that a women's body can always be improved. And this has become a public as well as private obsession because women have accepted its importance. But often hidden is the private anguish a woman experiences by not living up to the current norm of personal perfection.

Historical Perspective

Ayers (1958) notes there are historical shifts in ideals of fatness with a culture. However, both Ayers and Garland (1960) report that in general, past standards of beauty assess thinness much more negatively than contemporary norms dictate.

Beller (1977) notes that obesity has been recorded from paleolithic times via artwork. The women immortalized in Stone Age sculpture were fat. And it is likely that these women were perceived as aesthetically pleasing, if only because they were chosen as the artists' subjects.

However, according to Bruch (1973), the privileged classes of Western society have been preoccupied throughout history with concern about how to stay slim in the face of abundance. She states that ancient cultures, such as the Cretans, Spartans, Athenians, Greeks, and Romans scorned obesity. She compares Roman ladies to modern young women and states:

> They were literally starved to make them slim as reeds. The Romans are also known for the invention of the vomitorium that permitted them to indulge in excessive eating and then to relieve themselves, a method reinvented by modern college girls (Bruch 1973, p. 17)

Garland (1970) emphasizes that modified versions of extreme body types have often been desired simultaneously within cultures. For example, she states that the Greeks admired slimness, yet some of their goddesses were glorified as "mother earth" with solid, powerful, massive bodies. In fact, Bruch also acknowledges there were famous Greeks and Romans who were popular and fat, citing descriptions of some of their eating habits and body size.

During the Middle Ages various views were held on obesity. On the one hand, gluttony was deemed a venal sin. But obesity was also believed to be a sign of the "Grace of God" (Bruch 1973). In contrast to this view is one presented by Bell (1985) of seventeenth-century holy women recognized by the Roman Catholic Church as saints. He documents more than half as displaying clear signs of anorexia as a "response to the patriarchal social structures in which they were trapped" (Bell 1985, p. xii). Bell compares "holy anorexia" of the Catholic Middle Ages to "anorexia nervosa" of the twentieth century. Whether anorexia is holy or nervous depends on the culture in which control is sought by the anorexic. Bell (p. 20) states, "In both instances anorexia begins as the girl fastens onto a highly valued societal goal (bodily health, thinness, self-control in the twentieth century/spiritual health, fasting and self-denial in medieval Christendom."

Bell further notes that both holy anorexia and anorexia nervosa represent ideal states of their particular cultural milieu. In medieval Italy, holiness was held in high regard, while in contemporary Western society thinness is perceived as the feminine ideal.

There is an important historical implication for anorexia. Anorexia lost its appeal to medieval women, according to Bell, when it was no longer valued as a means to attain holiness. When female saints were defined as holy for their good works, apparently anorexia disappeared. Therefore, "...it follows that the incidence of anorexia nervosa will be reduced when the cultural ideals for feminine beauty and the 'liberated' woman are no longer connected with thinness" (Bell 1985, p. 190).

According to Boskind-White (1985), prior to the Victorian era a women's body was seen to reflect a "mother-earth" image. The primary identity of a woman was as mother; plumpness was acceptable and even symbolic of fertility, health, and survival. However, during Victorian times, the hour-glass figure became popular and dress was more seductive. Boskind-White hypothesizes that extremely restrictive clothing (tight corsets and rigid lacing) was created as a response to a new kind of American middle-class woman. Home and family were seen as separate from the world of work and money. As Hymowitz and Weissman (1978) point out, for the first time in America a class of women emerged who were supported by their husbands. No longer partners, they had become financially dependent. And, because of the "fashionable" cumbersome and inhibiting clothing, they were actually physically incapable of performing most work-related tasks. Therefore, by the 1800s bulk personified power, authority, and wealth for men, and women's size and roles were being dramatically redefined. Boskind-White (1985, p. 117) suggests "with the first great influx of European immigrants following the Victorian era, a robust female form increasingly came to be associated with being old, lower class, and intellectually inferior." Soon slimness became a sign of wealth and status for women.

The social class distinctions between affluent/thin and poor/fat continue today. Studies from the 1950s through the 1980s show obesity occurring seven times more frequently among lower-class than upper-class women (Goldblatt, Moore, and Stunkard 1973). In addition, obesity among women who dropped in social class is greater than among those who move upward in social status. Also, the longer a woman's family has been in America, the less likely she is to be fat (Moore, Stunkard, and Srole 1962).

From World War I through the 1950s, the ideal body shape for the majority of women was mature and sophisticated. Older women of the 1920s rejected the flapper as frivolous, and in the aftermath of the Depression, a fuller and heavier appearance was stylish. During the 1940s, sex goddesses like Rita Hayworth and Betty Grable led the trend toward a more seductive look. The 1950s era also encouraged sophistication, and women wore girdles and tight fitting bras (Boskind-White 1985).

Until the 1960s, fashion encouraged models to be mature and worldly looking. But with the advent of the "pop culture," a revolution occurred in fashion. According to Bender (1967), one half of the population was under 25 in America and England. And young aspiring designers in both countries were responding to the youth market.

Models like "Twiggy" (5'7", 92 lbs.) became fashion sensations in the 1960s. Adolescents began to starve themselves, imitating the body type of an underdeveloped young girl. However, unlike the flapper era, older women did not reject the values of the younger generation. Older women began to embrace youthfulness and pursue fashion trends such as "going braless" and wearing miniskirts. With the increased visibility of women's bodies, more and more women began dieting to conform to the new emaciated ideal (Chernin 1981).

During the 1970s, America was in a recession and many husbands' incomes were no longer sufficient. While the trend began during World War II, women were increasingly expected to contribute financially and new opportunities were becoming available. However, women had not been trained to compete. Most were unprepared to care for themselves.

In addition, divorce had become more accessible. Many women were on their own more than at any other time in American history. And their primary pursuit continued to be the attention of men. The diet industry cashed in on women's gullibility and anxiety. The diet industry made millions on various fad diets that promised male approval and magical answers to all of women's problems. Therefore, according to Boskind-White (1985), it did not matter what men actually said regarding feminine body size, the majority of women believed what they had been sold by the media (Orbach 1978).

Boskind-White (1985) further declares that it was almost inevitable that women's perfectionism and inner insecurities were fueled by the societal expectation of "superwomen." Women were expected to develop a career as well as maintain their duties as wives and mothers. And despite their lack of experience, they were expected to compete successfully with men in the job market.

According to Boskind-White, well-educated and liberated women of the 1980s are still drawn to the stereotypic female image presented by the media. And the media, dependent upon women as consumers, continue to encourage women's vigilance over their diet and body in order to make a profit.

Carol Gilligan's book, *In a Different Voice* (1982), offers feminist perspective arguing that all current theories of the psychology of women are limited. She states that current theory is primarily based on male phenomenology and development. She proposes that women have a basic need for intimacy and continually strive for direct personal connection.

If women possess innate needs for deep affiliation, then perhaps a society that encourages women to pursue power and an aggressive role may cause deep internal conflict. Following Gilligan's reasoning, women with eating disorders possess extremely strong feminine needs, and are strong, confident and assertive as a means of rebellion against male prerogatives and as a way to feel personally connected in a patriarchal society.

This position is supported by the work of Kim Chernin (1985) which takes a "dysfunctional" perspective on eating. Chernin asserts that the problem of "dysfunctional eating" conceals a problem of identity, which rests upon a hidden problem of traditional cultural rejection. According to Chernin (p. 186),

> Women today seem to be practicing genocide against themselves, waging a violent war against their female body precisely because there are no indications that the female body has been invited to enter culture.

Orbach (1978) identifies cultural demands of Western society on women to be slim and to fit certain preconceptions. She states that American culture emphasizes physical appearance as a central ingredient of a woman's identity. And according to messages from the media, a women's body is unacceptable as is and must be reshaped to fit the "ideal" body type. Orbach (1978, p. 21) states:

> Fat is a response to the many oppressive manifestations of a sexist culture. Fat is a way of saying "no" to powerlessness and self-denial, to a limiting sexual expression which demands that females look and act a certain way, and to an image of womanhood that defines a specific social role. Fat offends Western ideals of female beauty and, as such, every "overweight" women creates a crack in the popular culture's ability to make us mere products.

Almost a decade later, in *Hunger Strike* (1986), Susie Orbach declared that anorexia nervosa is the expression of every woman's plight (p. 19). Anorexia depicts the self-starved woman who is unable to feed or nurture herself, who must reject her own needs and desires, and who is too frightened and uncertain to find a means for authentic self-assertion (p. 114).

Orbach (1986, p. 24) argues that eating disorders are the "quintessential symbol of female oppression in a male-dominated culture." She claims that since women are brought up to nurture others rather than themselves, they are raised to expect less personal fulfillment. The primary result of this indoctrination is the legacy of mandatory self-sacrifice being passed on successfully to daughters by their mothers. Orbach's intention is not to accuse women of poor mothering. Rather, she insists the primary responsibility is due to the cultural dictates of a patriarchal society that demands women's subservience because of a deep fear of autonomous and self-sufficient women.

Cross-Cultural Perspective

Cross-cultural comparisons succinctly demonstrate that there are no universal standards of attractiveness (Rudofsky 1971), and that a predilection toward levels of fatness exists in all cultures, but commonly in opposite directions. Ford and Beach (1951) analyze sexual behavior and note that all cultures use body characteristics as a basis for judging attractiveness. They state that physical attributes are more important in females than males in establishing sexual desirability. In addition, they report that most societies view overweight females as more attractive than thin females.

They list thirteen cultures that are extremely attracted to fat women, and six that especially admire thin women. West (1974) analyzes the Karaqwe Kingdoms of East Africa where the harems of the king are composed of massively obese women who are considered the best sexual partners. Other cultures, like the Ekoi of Nigeria, send young girls away to fattening houses prior to marriage (Vander Zanden 1979). Cross culturally, eating behavior and body size preference take a variety of forms, depending on the cultural norms and on the conscious choices of people. However, Mayer (1968), Bruch (1973), and Friedman (1974), and others such as Stuart and Davis (1972), Stunkard (1976), and Brownell (1983a), note that the social stigma of nonnormative body size negatively affects individuals in most cultures. And in most instances, overconsumption has proved to be the exception, due most likely to the unavailability of a surplus food throughout most of the world.

The following correlational pattern is descriptive of American culture. However, it is applicable to all modern industrialized nations:

> With decreasing affluence, the constraint upon the development of obesity is a lack of food. With increasing affluence, fads and fashions exert the control. Information on the relationship of affluence to thinness, although less detailed, shows a pattern that is the mirror image of that for obesity (Bray 1979, p. 213).

Different ethnic groups have different cultures, and different cultures have different convictions about what, when, where, and how to eat (Bruch 1973). Starving people do not gain weight, no matter what ethnic group they originate from. Fat people do lose weight when they are systematically underfed, no matter what kind of climate or who their ancestors are. And at any given moment in history, some societies will be richer and therefore more apt to have food surpluses on hand than others, and will therefore offer greater opportunities to overfeed their citizens than those without. Starving people usually do not have the food available to them— if they did, they would eat. According to Bruch (1973), food refusal would be an ineffectual tool in a setting of poverty and food scarcity. She states that all her anorexic patients, regardless of which socioeconomic level they came from, had food available to them in abundance. Bruch (1973, p. 13) notes:

> No reports on anorexia nervosa have come from underdeveloped countries where there is still danger of widespread starvation or famine. It is worth mentioning that in the United States anorexia nervosa has not been reported in Negroes or members of other underprivileged groups. A disproportionately large percentage of patients with anorexia nervosa come from upper-class backgrounds, a few from the ranks of the super-rich. In other words, self-starvation is observed only under conditions of adequate food supply.

Thus, in developing countries of the world there is little likelihood for the occurrence of eating disorders similar to those which exist in our Western capitalistic society. For only in areas such as North America, Europe, and Japan, where people can afford the luxury of excessive food intake, do obesity, anorexia nervosa, and bulimarexia (bulimia) become a major public health problem (Beller 1977; Bray 1979; Bruch 1973).

In the United States, research consistently indicates that poor women are fatter and rich women are leaner, and fat decreases linearly with increasing income in women (Bray 1979). Studies in other cultures give different trends for weight and body size. In developing countries, there is a relationship between social factors and obesity which is completely opposite to that in Western urban society. According to Bray (1979), among adults in India, Latin America, and Puerto Rico, and among children in South China and the Philippines, an increased standard of living is associated with increased weight gain.

Ross and Mirowsky (1983) examined the relationship of social and cultural factors among Mexicans and Anglos at different social class levels. Among Mexicans, the overweight levels of men and women are fairly similar, with women being fatter than men. Among Anglos, however, the women are much thinner that the men. With increasing social class, overweight decreases for women, but social class has little effect on the obesity levels for men. They conclude that Mexican heritage affects weight. Possibly, norms concerning the social desirability and acceptability of thin women, which are so prevalent in Anglo culture, do not exist to such a degree among Mexicans. Stern, Pugh, Gaskill and Hazuda (1982), found that Mexican-Americans are more skeptical than Anglos about the desirability of losing weight and do not fully accept the American cultural ideal of thinness.

In addition, in a study of American Navaho children, affluence is directly related to the prevalence of obesity. The researchers also note that this finding is in sharp contrast to the relationship found in Western urban societies (Garb, Garb, and Stunkard 1975).

Demographic Correlates

The major demographic variables that relate to changes in the prevalence of eating disorders are those related to socioeconomic status. In general, whether one uses income, occupation, or educational level, the correlations with eating disorders are similar. Data from various studies (Bray 1979; Garn, Bailey, Cole, and Higgins 1977; Weil 1984) agree that there is an inverse correlation between socioeconomic status and obesity for adult and adolescent females; women of lower socioeconomic levels are more frequently obese than are women of higher socioeconomic levels. In addition, the reported incidences of bulimarexia (bulimia) and anorexia nervosa are positively correlated with socioeconomic status (Emmett 1985).

A demographic variable that also appears to correlate with eating behavior and weight is cultural separation. Weil (1984) concluded from his literature review that as individuals leave the culture that is "native" to them—either geographically or chronologically—they deviate increasingly from their original cultural norm. For example, if a group is fundamentally nonobese in its original location and time, removal from that culture, either physically or because the culture is altered, predisposes such "removed" persons to obesity. Weil (1984) cites several instances of this trend including American Indians, South African Blacks, and Samoans.

Other researchers study the concept of cultural similarity as it relates to eating patterns and body dimensions in successive familial generations. Extensive studies (Garn 1983; Garn, Bailey, and Cole 1980; Garn, Bailey, and Higgins 1980; Garn and Clark 1976), involving thousands of nuclear families, clearly demonstrates that the level of fatness follows family lines. However, very extensive recent studies of children adopted at an early age, of siblings, of husbands and wives, and of overweight persons and their pets, suggests that although fatness does follow family lines, it is learned, not inherited (Sims in Bray 1979).

The research of Garn, LaVelle, and Hopkins (1983) on adult children who maintain residence with their parents and on those who do not, shows some support for the role of cultural separation as a predisposing factor for eating periods (20 to 40 years), increasingly reflect similar eating habits and the shape of their parents.

Garn, LeVelle, and Pilkington (1984) note that the fatness change in one family member relates to that of another family member. It is clear that fat gain and fat loss go together in families even across generations—as between child and grandparent (precluding any genetic explanation) and across spousal lines (again precluding specific actions of the genes). They conclude that persons who live together as husbands and wives, parents and children, grandparents and grandchildren or as siblings resemble each other in fatness to significant degree. But, as demonstrated by young adult and older adult genetically unrelated adult pairs and child pairs living together, the influence of family on fatness is primarily in the actual living together. Therefore, obesity is acquired in the family context, in that obesity develops along a "largely-learned family line" (Garn, LeVelle, and Pilkington 1984, p. 33).

Body Size and Consumer Culture

The awareness of what constitutes a desirable body size reflects the biographical and sociocultural environment. A desirable body size is first defined in the eyes of the beholder (significant others) and then by self. For example, Allon (reported in Sobal 1984) notes that children are carefully taught to judge body shape by their significant others, such as parents, teachers, and peers, who communicate cultural attitudes about the meaning of such shapes.

Body image refers to a person's impression of his or her physical appearance and to the associated feelings. Reportedly, body image in eating disorder sufferers is characterized by the feeling that one's body is grotesque and detestable and that others view it with contempt and hostility (Brownell 1983a). This disturbance may lead to intense self-consciousness and to the notion that the world views them with disapproval. Consequently, persons with body-image disparagement tend to be withdrawn, shy, and socially immature (Brownell 1983b).

Eating disorders are most commonly attributed to a woman's desire to change her size because she feels uncomfortable with her body (Orbach 1978; Millman 1980; Boskind-White and White 1983). Society, via the media, continually bombards women with the message that they are unattractive, unacceptable physically, as well as inadequate. Women are given the dictum that they must nurture others by means of providing hearty and healthy meals and snacks, but must deny themselves this same means of oral satisfaction. A woman who compulsively eats, purges, or starves her body has absorbed this message and is mirroring its relation to her through her eating behavior and her body.

Currently, standards for weight are so narrowly set and promoted, that women who fail to attain and maintain these weight requirements are easily made to feel inadequate. The image created is that the female who is even a few pounds overweight is at a significant disadvantage in the interpersonal relationship "market" (Allon 1976).

A study by Kallen and Doughty (1984) demonstrates that even among a group of college students who are below the national norms of weight for height, a substantial proportion of the females think they are overweight. In this particular instance, even the underweight females reported, that they weigh too much. This self perception of overweight, which is only loosely related to actual weight per inch of height, has a negative influence for these collegian women on self-esteem and on courtship behavior. At the same time, men who perceive themselves to be underweight or overweight also suffer a social disadvantage in courtship, reinforcing the concept of the society communicating an idealized body conformation to both males and females. However, physical attractiveness is much more important socially for females than for males. Interestingly, Kallen and Doughty state that among women, it appears that there is no such thing as being too thin. Being heavy and feeling fat has a negative effect on participation in the courtship system, and probably on eventual marriage. They noted that virgins with a disvalued body type (overweight) were apt to date less than those with more valued physiques. Finally, for men, social competence was associated with coital experience and not with body type, while the opposite was true for women. "It would appear that the source of social competence for men is associated with what they can do, while for women, it is still highly tied to how they appear" (Kallen and Doughty 1984; p. 113). Paradoxically, studies of fatness in marriage cohorts reveal that for most couples weight is not a major criterion for courtship and marriage (Sobal 1984). In this culture Sobal proposes that the importance of body size may be minor for some in the selection of a mate, while others put extreme pressure on themselves to be thin in order to attract a marriage partner.

One reason female shape is valued so highly in terms of marriageability is that women are treated as a commodity (Beller

1977). Traditionally, fatter women are seen as healthier, more fertile, and more adaptable to cold, while in modern industrial societies weather and disease factors play a smaller role and thin women are more highly valued.

Millman (1980) notes there is a double standard in Western societies, where fatness is more salient in women than men. This leads to differential concerns about being overweight. Douvan and Adelson (1966) allege that during adolescence there is a greater preoccupation with physical appearance in girls because self-esteem in girls is based on popularity and appearance while boys focus on mastery of skills and achievements for self-esteem.

The preceding research indicates that despite any genetic and biochemical determinants, "eating disorders" appear to be predominantly under societal control. Eating disorders are not forms of disease; they are labels fostered by an insidious socialization process that prepares women to accept weakness, sickness, and victimization. Becker (1963; p. 9) notes that "social groups create deviance by making the rules." Thus, the "collective definition" is a process of labeling by which some persons or groups impose their rules on others. Ultimately, who will be defined as deviant by the society, and for what behavior, is a "question of political and economic power" (Becker 1963, p. 17).

Incidence Symptomotolgy and Treatment Outcome

It is estimated that approximately 50 percent of American women spend their entire lives unsuccessfully attempting to control their bodies' shape (Bennett and Gurin 1982; Chernin 1981; Orbach 1978; and Sussman 1956). In our culture, Bruch (1973) observes, to achieve the status of beauty, especially by members of the upper and middle classes, many women wage a continuous battle against their bodies.

Widespread negative concern with obesity has begun to develop only within the last 150 years (Schwartz 1984). And most of the research into the social causes and consequences of obesity has been within the last 25 to 30 years. Government estimates of the prevalence of overweight are reported at approximately 38 percent of the population deviating by 20 percent or more from desirable weight (U.S. Health Examination Survey 1960-62 and Health and Nutrition Examination Survey 1971-74, 1979). Beller (1977, p. 10) also notes that although there is a 40 percent obesity rate, there is 40 to 70 percent of the American population preoccupied with weight and weight control measures. As an example of how serious this issue has become for the medical community, the following quote is taken from the U.S. Department of Health, Education, and Welfare, NIH Publication No. 79-359.

> ...obesity is a hazard to health and a detriment to well-being ...one of the most important medical and public health problems of our time... (Bray 1979, p. 1).

According to Beeson and McDermott (1979), 30 percent of American males and 40 percent of American females are twenty pounds or more overweight. These researchers insist that obesity has become one of our culture's most important public health problems, and it is a concomitant of many chronic diseases.

Some of the medical hazards of obesity are as follows: adult-onset diabetes, menstrual abnormalities, reproductive problems, heart size and function, arthritis, gout, hypertension, endometrial carcinoma, atherosclerotic disease, gallbladder disease, and death (Rimm and White 1979). Others include renal problems, surgical risk, complications during pregnancy, elevated levels of low-density lipoprotein cholesterol, hyperlipidemia, and carbohydrate intolerance (Brownell 1983a). In addition, Brownell comments that the psychological and social consequences of obesity may be as serious as the medical hazards.

However, in contrast to the above statements, Gordon and Tobias (1984) allege that a variety of studies published in the past ten years have found that the health hazards of overweight have been overstated. "And yet, ordinary people are still being instructed by physicians to lose weight in order to stay well" (Bennett and Gurin 1982, Chap. 5, reported by Gordon and Tobias 1984, p. 74). Millman (1980, p. xi) states concerning the obese,

> especially is she is a woman, she probably suffers more from the social and psychological stigma attached to obesity than she does from the actual physical condition. In a wide variety of ways she is negatively defined by her weight and excluded from full participation in the ranks of the normal.

While Sours (1980, reported in Schur 1984) notes that anorexia nervosa had a long psychiatric history, it has been an object of greatly increasing attention and discussion in recent times. He states that anorexia

> now affects tens of thousands of young women of high school and college age and appears to be increasingly rapid in most counties where there is an affluent, well-educated segment of society (Sours 1980, p. 63).

Anorexia nervosa is primarily a disturbance of adolescent girls. Usually the onset is between the ages of eleven and fifteen; about one-fifth of the cases arise after mid-adolescence. This onset distribution is also true for male patients, but the frequency for males compared to females is one in twenty (Sours 1979). Although there is clinical agreement concerning an increase in the incidence of anorexia nervosa in the United States, Britain, Japan, and in continental Europe, there are few supportive statistics. Sours cites only one study where "the risk was fifty to seventy-five per 100,000" (p. 572). Further, he doubts whether any epidemiological study could produce accurate statistics due to physician underreporting; confusion of criteria for assessment; various groups that manifest the behavior but do not lose control and require treatment (i.e., ballerinas and gymnasts); and denial and/or concealment by anorexics themselves. Regarding incidence rates of anorexia and bulimia, Chernin (1985, p. 13) claims, "In fact, there is, at present, a major epidemic of eating disorders in the United States." She states that anorexia is present in 1 in 250 girls between sixteen and eighteen years old, and cites other estimates "as high as 1 in 100." In addition, less than eight percent of anorexics are male, therefore, anorexia is primarily a female disorder. Further, she notes that one in five college-age women suffer from bulimia, and presents these figures as conservative estimates.

The symptoms of anorexia nervosa include starvation, amenorrhea, constipation, preoccupation with food, abdominal pain, intolerance to cold, and vomiting. The physical complications are hypotension, hypothermia, dry skin, lanugo type hair, bradycardia, edema, systolic murmur and petechiae. These systems and physical signs are outlined in Warren and Van de Wiele's (1973) case study for forty-two patients.

Although at least one research team (Boskind-White and White 1983) has labeled the binge-purge cycle as a separate disease titled bulimarexia, others, such as Schur (1984) profess this cycle is special version of anorexia, termed bulimia. These cases involve periodic eating "binges" followed by some manner of purging the system, usually induced vomiting. One specialist states, "The gorging-vomiting group of anorexia nervosa patients makes up at least 25 percent of all cases of the disorder" (Sours 1980, p. 245). Brody (1981, p. C1) commented,

> Psychotherapists at eating disorder clinics around the country say the secretive phenomenon, which nearly always starts with a stringent diet to lose weight, is now epidemic on college campuses.

The physical appearance of bulimic and anorexic patients reflects their qualitative and quantitative nutritional intake. Whereas anorexic behavior and weight loss usually draw attention to the patient's "problem," even if the actual diagnosis remains elusive, most bulimics have been purging themselves for months or years before discovery. In one recent study of college freshmen, 4.5 percent of the women and 4 percent of the men admitted bulimic behavior (Pyle, Mitchell, Eckert, Halvorson, Neuman, and Goff 1983). These bulimics maintain themselves at, or even below, ideal body weight and consider purging to be absolutely necessary to achieve any semblence of desirable body weight.

Because most bulimics conceal their eating patterns, it is usually less obvious than anorexia nervosa, which has more clear-cut physical signs as it progresses. One report estimates that bulimia occurs in as many as half of the patients who suffer from anorexia nervosa (Fairburn 1984) and a minority of such patients also use vomiting, laxatives, or diuretics to control their weight (Fairburn 1984). In addition, current research indicates bulimarexia is increasing rapidly. Estimates among college students range from 3.8 percent (Stangler and Printz 1980) to 13 percent (Halmi, Falk, and Schwartz 1982).

Bulimics' apparent external physical normality, however,

> may belie subtle physical changes such as dental erosion from gastric acid or parotid swelling. Serious electrolyte losses from the individual or combined effects of laxatives, diuretics, or vomiting (or a superimposed

gastroenteritis) render these patients potassium-depleted, with little margin to prevent hypokalemia (Spack 1985, p. 5).

Additionally, at some point of decreased serum potassium, the contractility of myocardial tissue is affected and death due to arrhythmia or "total asystole" may occur (Keys, Brozek, Henschel, Mickelson, and Taylor 1950).

Currently, the treatment of eating disorders is a difficult undertaking. It is usually time consuming, frequently frustrating, often very expensive, and it seldom guarantees success. Popular treatments cover the entire spectrum of psychological services. Patients are treated using psychoanalysis, cognitive psychotherapy, behavior therapy, gestalt and existential psychology, group psychotherapy, and family therapy. There are hospital treatment programs using milieu techniques and behavior modification. Psychopharmocologic treatment may also be included in all of the above. There are also countless self-help organizations, each with its own ideology and program of recovery for compulsive overeaters/undereaters. This plethora of treatment modalities clearly demonstrates a lack of a uniformly effective treatment.

While many therapeutic approaches have been proposed for eating disorders, they have only been effective in a small minority of patients. In studies using psychodynamic, familial, group and behavioral techniques with anorexia and bulimic patients, none has yet been shown to be effective in a controlled study, and even the number of available uncontrolled studies remains small and equivocal (Pope and Hudson 1985). In fact, a recent review of outcome studies of anorexia nervosa (Agras and Kraemer 1984) concludes that in the past fifty years, there has been no significant advance in the treatment of anorexia. Krieshok and Karpowitz (1988) examine the literature and treatment guidelines for obesity. They allege that regardless of numerous treatment programs available, no effective "cure" has been developed. Stunkard (1980) estimates that no more than 25 percent of obese persons lose 20 pounds, and no more than 5 percent of those who participate in some form of treatment program lose 40 pounds. And, according to Brownell (1983a, p. 820) "...a person is more likely to recover from most forms of cancer than from obesity."

Medicalization of Eating Disorders

According to Conrad and Schneider (1980, p. 285), "Medicalization increases directly with its economic profitability." They note that new markets for large industries create corporate profits from medicalizing deviance. In addition, specialized groups are created by control agents, who receive an income based on promotion and supporting the medicalization of deviance (i,e., staff wages). Finally certain corporate interests are indirectly supported. For example, the health insurance industry affects and is affected by medicalizing deviance.

In order for a deviance designation to be accepted as a medical issue, individuals are needed who will take an active role in the creation and maintenance of defining a behavior as deviant and a medical problem. Becker (1963) calls these individuals "moral entrepreneurs," while Conrad and Schneider (1980) refer to them as "champions." Moral entrepreneurs, champions, and special interest groups are actively involved in the creation and acceptance of a new deviance designation. Conrad and Schneider further state that both medical and nonmedical interest groups conceptualize the deviant or the deviant's behavior as a medical problem in order to extend the arena of medical social control.

Gordon and Tobias (1984) claim that in our technologically and medically oriented culture, the knowledge of the common people is to a great extent influenced by experts. In the case of eating disorders, which are defined as a medical problem, many health care professionals lay claim to being recognized experts on "appropriate" weight and eating behavior (Bray 1979; Brownell 1983a; Krieshok and Karpowitz 1988; Stuart and Davis 1972; and Stunkard 1958, 1976).

Therefore, moral entrepreneurs in the field of eating disorders may come from two distinct categories of individuals. There are those inside the medical profession and those who support the nonmedical interest of labeling women as having an eating disorder. The medical professional group is composed of researchers and physicians either independently operating or working for an institution. They are dependent on eating disorders being viewed as a disease. For example, the American Society of Bariatric Physicians promotes defining and treating obesity as an illness.

The nonmedical moral entrepreneurs utilize the information from the medical professional group to support their own interests in promoting eating disorders as a medical illness. There are industries (e.g., the restaurant and food industry; the fashion industry; the health/fitness industries), professional groups (e.g., Anorexia Nervosa Aid Society; National Council on Obesity), lay organizations (National Association to Aid Fat Americans; Fat Liberation Front), government bureaucracies (e.g., Task Force on the Definitions, Criteria and Prevalence of Obesity in the Department of Health, Education and Welfare), commercial enterprises (e.g. Weight Watchers International; Nutri System Weight Loss Centers; Holiday Spa Health Clubs; Pritikin Centers), and self-help groups (e.g. Overeaters Anonymous; TOPS, an acronym for Take Off Pounds Sensibly; 3D's which is likewise an acronym for Diet, Discipline and Discipleship). Conrad and Schneider (1980, p. 269) claim that special interest groups such as those listed above "have a direct interest be it economic, moral, administrative, or therapeutic, in the adoption of the medical prespective of deviance." One such special interest group, Overeaters Anonymous (OA), has a major influence on staff and patients on SED (Section on Eating Disorders). Therefore, it is important to briefly discuss OA's history and philosophy. In America, there is a tendency for people to organize informal groups to achieve ends that are the usual responsibility of formalized institutions. This proclivity is demonstrated by the organization of patients to cope with common illnesses. Patient self-help groups, pioneered by Alcoholics Anonymous, are attracting great numbers of persons suffering from an increasing variety of conditions.

One of the largest and most effective of these group is Overeaters Anonymous, a twenty-three year old organization with an estimated membership of 190,000 in over nine thousand groups which meet weekly in the United States and other parts of the world. Overeaters Anonymous began when three women took the principles of Alcoholics Anonymous and adapted them to fit overeaters. OA is not a diet club; it does not advertise, there are no frozen OA meals or snacks, no diet plans, no weight-ins, no dues or fees. OA is dedicated to helping people conquer the underlying cause of fat: the disease of compulsive overeating. And thus by labeling deviant eating behaviors as a disease, OA joined the ranks of moral entrepreneurs.

Eating Disorders Clinics

Until recently, traditional public health efforts in the field of weight control and eating behavior management were on an individual doctor to patient basis. However, with the advent of the eating disorder clinic, medical agencies are using a broader-scale effort to reinforce the concept of medical intervention to provide improved personal health.

Political and economic influences dealing with the issue of control of women's bodies are compounded by the medical claims that highlight the hazards of eating disorders. Private hospital treatment programs have, therefore, emerged as a solution to individuals efforts to control their eating behavior. Eating disorder clinics are accepted by many medical and nonmedical interest groups as an appropriate treatment approach because of two profit-making incentives.

First, the increasingly availability of medical insurance to cover psychiatric treatment in hospital settings clearly demonstrates how the policy-making of third-party payers can dramatically affect what the medical community labels deviant and how the deviant should be treated. Because out-patient care for eating disorders, such as overeating, is minimally reimbursed by current coverage provisions of most insurance companies, all patients are given the psychiatric diagnosis of depression in in-patient facilities such as SED in order to receive maximum insurance benefits.

Second, the profit incentives of doctors and institutions make it more profitable to provide fully reimbursed inpatient treatment rather than limited reimbursed out-patient intervention. For example, the administrative assistant of SED disclosed to me the following 1986 figures pertaining to types of treatment rendered:

> It is nineteen hundred dollars for out-patient (treatment) and insurance usually pays fifty percent. In-patient runs eighteen to twenty-four thousand, but insurance pays eighty to ninety percent...and that's for about forty-two days on in-patient.

Future Frontiers of Eating Disorders

It is likely we will continue to witness a burgeoning awareness of the prevalence and severity of eating disorders into the next century. The media, academic conferences, literature, clinics and self-help organizations are vigorously exploring the myriad aspects of dysfunctional eating patterns and their consequences. Cases in point are two researchers in the eating disorder field who currently are making claims for broadening the existing diagnostic categories. Ratliff and McVoy (1988) state that the *Diagnostic and Statistical Manuel, III-Revised* (DSM-III-R) should be expanded where eating disorders are concerned. They discuss the diagnosis, assessment and treatment of what they term atypical eating disorders, mentioning six disorders and implying others may soon be identified. The Ratliff and McVoy atypical eating disorders list follows:

1. Phobic Eating Disorder meets the DSM-III-R criteria for a simple phobia and includes the fears of swallowing food, contaminated food, and nausea.

2. Laxative Dependency Disorder does not fit the criteria for bulimia nervosa and deserves a listing of its own. The patient regularly ingests propulsive laxitives in increasing amounts and frequencies over time and experiences physical symptoms and anxiety when atttempting to discontinue usage.

3. With Obese Anorexia the patient does not meet DSM-III—R criteria for anorexia nervosa but does exhibit a morbid fear of weight gain, significant and persistent weight loss, and refusal to deviate from restricted eating patterns.

4. Conversion Vomiting meets DSM-III-R criteria for conversion hysteria with the conversion aimed primarily toward eating disorder symptoms: uncontrolled, involuntary vomiting and appetite loss. The patient often experiences significant weight loss as a result. Symptoms serve to manage stress, avoid stressful situations, and gain attention from significant others.

5. Psychotic-Induced Eating Disorders meet the DSM-III-R criteria for schizophrenia and schizoaffective disorder. Irregular eating patterns and weight loss (and obsession with both) are present. These disorders are a result of the psychosis, rather than the reverse, but this may not be apparent until the patient returns to normal eating patterns. A fear of fat will accompany the patient's return to normal weight.

6. Hyperphagia, out-of-control eating that leads to obesity, occurs in response to stress. These patients are severly obese and 50 percent or more over their ideal weight. They compulsively overeat or eat in binges, experience feelings of disgust or low self-worth as a result, and reveal an observable association between their eating behaviors and emotional states or between their weight gain and certain events (Ratliff and McVoy 1988, p. 10)

If these expanding deviance labels for eating disorders are to be formally accepted by society, the next step of claims-making (Conrad and Schneider 1980) must occur. If moral entrepreneurs, champions, and special interest groups promote and politicalize these claims, the field of eating disorders may be expanded to a much larger medical social control arena by appealing to medical and nonmedical interest groups with profit as a primary motivator.

To summarize, this study focuses on how labeling has effectively changed eating from a field of behavior into a field of medical intervention. My analysis contributes to the research of labeling theory by demonstrating a complexity and layering effect that has previously been absent in the sociological literature.

One of the primary assumptions in labeling theory has been that there exists only one "master status" label which originates from one source with only one effect on the individual. I analyze several levels of labels derived from a combination of sources beginning with the DSM-III medical-macro label of psychiatric depression, moving to the deviance designation of "compulsive overeater" in the self-help/Overeaters Anonymous group classification, and finally, to the micropolitical level of the actual staff interaction labels. Each of these levels of labeling carries a master-status stigmatization of the patient depending on who is doing the deviant defining and who makes up the audience.

SED patients go through three stages during hospitalization in order to be transformed from "sick" to "recovered." These phases are entering, working toward recovery, and discharge. Staff use two mechanisms of control to facilitate this process. These are labeling and emotion management. Women on SED use storytelling throughout their career as patients in response to staff and to legitimize (for themselves) their struggle through this process. Chapter II discusses the setting and methods. Chapter III analyzes entering the system and emphasizes the multilevel labeling process. Chapter IV deals with working the program. During this liminal phase of "getting better," patients struggle with managing their emotions in order to display a "recovering" identity to staff. Chapter V analyzes the various social control mechanisms staff use to affect the expression of emotion which they assume controls eating behavior. Chapter VI explores the usefulness of storytelling. Of special importance is how staff use patient's stories to subjectively measure recovery during the discharge phase of treatment. And finally, Chapter VII gives some conclusions of this study and suggests areas of further sociological exploration.

Chapter II

The Study and its Methods

The setting for this enthnography is an inpatient ward of a hospital designed to treat patients who are hospitalized for an eating disorder.[1] The SED is a unit within a "for-profit" medical facility I refer to as the Provider Treatment Hospital (PTH). It is located in a metropolitan area. PTH is a freestanding facility owned by a public company I call the Health Provider Corporation (HPC). HPC engages in the development, marketing, and management of programs for the treatment of chemical dependency and psychiatric disorders. At the time of my study, HPC had over one hundred contractual agreements with the independent general hospitals and operated or participated in the operation of over ten facilities nationwide representing over one thousand available beds. The corporate net earnings during this period were will over twelve million dollars.

PTH is licensed as a psychiatric hospital. The PTH facility offers three types of behavioral medicine programs. It provides chemical dependency, adolescent and eating disorders treatment in three physically separate wings of the same, one-story building. Each wing is considered a separate autonomous unit within the facility, having its own separate staff, with the exception of the staff psychiatrist, who is actively involved with all three programs. The eating disorders program treats individuals suffering from anorexia nervosa, bulimia, and obesity. Medical staff give each patient entering the program a physical examination and nutritional assessment. Additional diagnostic and psychiatric evaluations are performed by the psychiatrist and clinical social worker when necessary. On SED, each patient's treatment is overseen by the staff psychiatrist, who also directs the management of any attendant medical or psychological problem of the patient.

The SED is a thirty-bed unit offering both residential and out-patient medical care. The occupancy rate during my fieldwork (1982-1983) was about 40 percent. The typical length of stay was four to six weeks and the cost of treatment was approximately $340.00 per day. Therefore the total cost to the patient was estimated to be between $10,000 to $15,000.

Staff consisted of four paraprofessional therapists, two nurses, the staff psychiatrist, a clinical social worker, the clinical director of the program and myself (a clinical intern). All were female except the psychiatrist. Of the four paraprofessional counselors, only one had achieved a bachelor's degree and one was in the process of obtaining an associate degree in education. These women were hired because they had experience in OA which qualified them for the job, and/or were personal friends of the clinical director. They did not have licenses to do family therapy or alcohol counseling.

In addition to the staff, others involved in day-to-day clinic life include the immediate families of these patients; the administrative personnel, referring physicians and EAP reps (Employee Assistance Program representatives from the patient's employment); and members of the organization of Overeaters Anonymous. The OA members are referred to as "sponsors," and have demonstrated some success in areas such as food control or spiritual growth. Staff expect a patient to call her sponsor, usually on a daily basis, to report on successes and failures accrued throughout the day. Sponsors from OA very rarely have physical contact with patients, until the patients are given aftercare status. At this point, the sponsor and the patient are likely to meet weekly before or after an OA meeting to discuss the patient's continuing progress toward recovery.

Medical insurance covers the vast majority of the patients who are given the primary diagnosis of depression using DSM-III. Staff assert that the diagnosis of a major depression is essential because "insurance carriers will not cover eating disorders but they will cover depression. And all of these (patients) are depressed about their weight, aren't they?"

The staff responded to telephone inquiries with the following information concerning insurance coverage. The unit secretary generally told the prospect that "usually insurance covers 80 percent of $10,000." The patient would have to "pay 20% and it was likely that the total bill would be around $10,000 to $12,000. You'd end up owing approximately $2,000." The secretary then informed a prospective patient that, "The physician isn't part of the hospital bill, and that fee is usually $500 to $700 per patient...also the business office want $250 downpayment for security purposes."

The vast majority of patients are upper-middle class Caucasian women who have an extensive history of compulsively overeating food. There were, in fact, only three male patients during the term of my internship. Most patients were adults with an average age in the mid-thirties, although there was an occasional admission of a teenager. The youngest patient on the unit was 14 years old, while the oldest was 58 years old. All of these patients voluntarily committed themselves because they believed there was no alternate means to successfully change their eating behavior or physical condition. Some, however, were hospitalized under duress from their respective employers. For example, Patti, an airline stewardess for a major airline corporation, claimed:

> I used to weigh 110 pounds three years ago. But now I weigh 135 pounds and I got put on probation. I am so angry at the airlines for doing this to me. I had no choice but to be here...I was weighed every two weeks and I was told that I would get suspended if I didn't lose one and a half pounds per week. I couldn't do it on my own, and they told me if I didn't lose the weight, they would fire me. So they put me in here...It's a reality for all my friends (obsession with weight control)...we have three stews in Chicago in the hospital for anorexia, they are so scared of losing their jobs.

The social interaction during which most of the information for this ethnography was gathered occurred at staff meetings, in the family therapy sessions, during meals, informal chatting between sessions, on staff/patient outings, and while charting patient records. Because I was a staff member, I saw more of the backstage talk among the staff. I was also aware there was a separate patient culture. However, that was not my focus in this study.

Patients are involved in activities from 7 a.m. to 9 p.m. (see Figure 1: Activities Chart). They receive psychological counseling, behavior modification, nutrition education, exercise programming, family therapy and aftercare treatment, which involves the support network of Overeaters Anonymous (OA).

Figure 1. Activities Chart

SUNDAY	MONDAY	TUESDAY	WEDNESDAY	THURSDAY	FRIDAY	SATURDAY
7-8 Wake-up Shower & Dress	7-8 Wake-up Shower & Dress	7-8 Wake-up Shower & Dress	7-8 Wake-up Shower & Dress	7-8 Wake-up Shower & Dress	7-8 Wake-up Shower & Dress	7-8 Wake-up
8-8:45 Breakfast	8-8:45 Breakfast	8-8:45 Breakfast	8-8:45 Breakfast	8-8:45 Breakfast	8-8:45 Breakfast	8-8:45 Breakfast
9-9:30 Free Time	9-10 Com. Meeting	9-10:30 Exercise	9-10. O.T.	9-10:30 Exercise	8:45-9:45 Free Time	9-10 Free Time
9:30	10:15-11:45 Exercise	10:30-11 Shower	10:15-11:45 Exercise	10:30-11 Shower	10-1:15	10
Outside Activity	11:45-12:15 Shower	11-12 Dialog	11:45-12:15 Shower	11-12 Big Book Study	Picnic & Outside Meeting	Outside Activity
	12:15-1:15 Gentle Eating	12:15-1:15 Gentle Eating	12:15-1:15 Gentle Eating	12:15-1:15 Gentle Eating		
	1:15-2:45 Group	1:15-2:45 Group Therapy	1:15-2:45 Group	1:15-2:45 Group Therapy	1:30-3:00 Group	
	3-4 Education	3-4 Education/ Nutrician	3-4 Education/Film	3-4 Education	3:15-4:15 Step Study	
	4:15-4:45 Homework	4:15-4:45 Homework	4:15-4:45 Homework	4:15-4:45 Homework	4:15-4:45 Homework	
4:45 Dinner	4:45 Dinner	4:45 Dinner	4:45 Dinner	4:45 Dinner	4:45 Dinner	4:45 Dinner
6-7 Free Time	6 Family/ Aftercare Therapy	6-7 Visiting	6 Family/ Aftercare Therapy	6-7 Free Time/ Assignments	6-8:30 Nutrition	6 Free Time
7-9 Visiting		7-10 Outside OA Mtg.		7:30-9 In House OA Mtg.		

32

In addition to the regularly scheduled activities on the unit, a patient may be awarded a "pass" by the staff. Passes are authorized permission to be outside the unit for a specific therapeutic reason and for a strictly limited period of time. Staff usually assign passes during weekend hours. Most passes are for family visits or some other therapeutic purpose, such as a massage, an OA meeting "on the outside" with a sponsor or friend, or a "date" with a spouse for an intimate encounter.

In addition to the full time schedule for patients, their behavior is also tightly regimented. The SED program parallels Goffman's (1961) description of a "total institution"—which is a place of residence where individuals are isolated from society for an appreciable period of time. Orientation into SED also has characteristics of Van Gennep's (1960) separation phase where individuals are exposed to resocialization experiences that systematically seek to strip away their old roles and identities and fashion new ones. During this phase on the unit, individuals are separated from family members and friends who provide networks of support for old eating habits. Patients are made vulnerable to institutional control and discipline by being deprived of personal items and privileges. Patient's contact with the outside world is discouraged, and outsiders' attempts to contact patients is monitored. There are no personal radios, TVs, newspapers, or any literature other than hospital-approved books and pamphlets. Phone call are restricted as to place and time. For example, each patient was permitted only one phone call a day for a three to five minute conversation. A staff member was present in the room for the complete conversation.[2] Staff meetings are customarily held for two hours every Wednesday afternoon in an empty group therapy room. All on-duty staff members are present. Charts of all active patients are available for documentation. The first hour of staffing is normally a formal event focusing on charting information regarding prognosis and treatment plans for patients. Each new patient is assigned a "primary" therapist (one of the paraprofessionals), who is responsible for updating the chart and documenting evidence of recovery or relapse. Every paraprofessional counselor is held accountable for approximately three or four patients in any one week.

When all charting is complete, the staff psychiatrist traditionally leaves the meeting. The time remaining in the second hour is then likely to evolve into an informal forum for complaints against the administration and comments and stories regarding resistant or difficult patients.

Throughout my entire internship, there were only three occasions when a person from outside the hospital milieu actually attended a staff meeting. All three of these visiting outsiders were EAP representatives wanting to know prognosis and projected length of hospitalization for the particular patient they were monitoring. Private physicians did call the unit to get periodic patient reports but never came to staffings, although they were always formally invited.

Private doctors are only permitted minimal control of their patients in SED. Ordinarily staff are in complete control of patient care. The typical reason for the doctors' lack of involvement on the ward is that the staff psychiatrist is listed as the doctor "on record." Therefore, the private doctors are not likely to be reimbursed for hospital visits. "So they leave us alone, and that's fine with us...most of them don't know anything [about eating disorders] anyway..." claimed one of the paraprofessional counselors.

The family group sessions are provided for the benefit of patients and their families. Staff advise family members that they are "co-addicted to the compulsive eater." From the staff's perspective, family members actions toward the patient are really *reactions* to the deviant behavior and status of the compulsive overeater. A frequent remark by staff to family members was "You can't help yourselves. You have to respond that way because you are co-addicted...you are dependent on them [patients]. And you have to accept that you are just as sick as they [patients] are." Staff require immediate family to attend group therapy two nights a week and a vast majority of family members comply. Staff ritualistically inform the patient's family during admission:

> Your loved one has an 80 percent chance of recovering if you are involved in treatment. This is a family problem and her disease affects you, too. You are a co-compulsive overeater and your behavior supports her addiction. And if you don't get involved [in therapy] she only has a twenty percent chance of recovery.

Because staff state that family therapy sessions are mandatory, children as young as seven years attend these sessions.

Four groups are held simultaneously during the first session of family therapy treatment. Each group is composed of at least one staff member and individual family members. No two members of the same family are permitted in the same group, unless the family is composed of more than four members. In that case, the children are usually assigned together. The second session consists of an educational presentation by a staff member concerning some aspect of the eating disorder syndrome. All family members, patients, and staff attend. The final session is multiple family therapy. Family members are together as a unit and combine with other family units. This arrangement is based on a prior staff evaluation of the most appropriate placement for each family. Four groups are conducted simultaneously and are facilitated by a minimum of one staff member. No switching among members or families concerning placement within a particular group occurs once treatment begins.

After discharge for SED, patients and family members attend aftercare meetings for two nights a week for a period of approximately six weeks. Staff monitor follow-up via telephone calls and letters to those not attending the meetings on a regular basis. Staff believe that observation of patients working with other family members in family group therapy sessions is important for diagnosis and treatment. In this setting, the staff provide the patients with ample opportunities to practice assertively stating their needs and desires. The counselor also encourages the other patients and family members to give advice, support, and encouragement for any attempt by the patient to deal more effectively with a particular problem.

Staff describe SED as a program of recovery for people who are afflicted with a "major health problem" labeled "dysfunctional eating." It is modeled closely upon Overeaters Anonymous and its parent organization of Alcoholics Anonymous which regards dysfunctional eating as a compulsive disease that is serious, self-destructive, and potentially life-threatening (Overeaters Anonymous 1980). Like alcoholism, staff view dysfunctional eating as a manifestation of a progressive physical, psychological, and spiritual disease that is never cured but might be "arrested" through strict adherence to the treatment (and the OA) program.

The clinical director takes several measures which guarantee that the SED philosophy will reflect the influence of Overeaters

Anonymous (OA). First, the clinical director hires only staff who are current members of OA and are actively supportive of the OA philosophy. Second, the clinical director constantly encourages staff to share their autobiographical "stories" of personal recovery from the disease (the twelfth step assignment from OA)—in order to present successful role models for the patients. Third, the clinical director also directs the staff to minimize differences and maximize universality with and among the patients. Staff tell patients, "We all have the same disease. We all know where you are coming from...we've all been there before." This dictum is applied regardless of gross differences in physical manifestations of the "disease." As an example of the universality policy, weight loss is not stressed by staff as a major benefit of this therapeutic treatment, although it is the primary concern of most patients throughout hospitalization. Interestingly, obesity research cited earlier shows that the vast majority of treatment approaches are markedly unsuccessful at weight reduction. Because the SED program was in operation for only a few months prior to my joining the staff, and the clinical director was acutely aware of the dismal success rate, a manifest function of downplaying weight loss was to minimize patient discouragement while simultaneously maximizing rapport.

In addition, staff avoid indirectly compromising the SED program by drawing attention to the low rates of successful weight loss. During admission orientations, counselors almost automatically said to new patients and their families: "Everyone in here is special, but no one is unique. Ninety percent of the patients who leave here recover." Therefore, although patients are weighed upon admission and at termination of treatment, in general the staff policy is to downplay weight. A moderate change in weight (either a gain or loss depending on the individual's particular type of problem) which is the most common treatment outcome, is seldom commented upon by the staff. However, when a patient reveals to her peers a major weight loss (over forty pounds) this disclosure results in that patient receiving substantial accolades from peers as well as from the staff. For example, a patient named Linda gives her final "goodbye" speech at the end of her treatment during an education group meeting. She announced she had lost 43 pounds and received applause and a standing ovation from many of the staff and patients.

While weight loss is usually not stressed, staff expect patients to exhibit a substantial change in eating patterns which staff perceive as a sign of recovery. In order for the patients to reorganize and change their existing eating habits, there is a twofold approach to food retraining. One approach is essentially educational. Once a week, for an hour, the patients meet with a nutritionist and discuss meal planning, nutrients, metabolism, and other food related topics. One evening a week, for approximately two and a half hours, the patients and any interested family members gather for another session with the nutritionist. This group is designed primarily for problem solving, support, and menu planning involving a patient's return to the home environment.

The second approach utilizes behavior modification techniques titled "Gentle Eating." Gently eating is a universally practiced ritual involving the patients during lunch time four days a week. Staff teach patients how to carefully and slowly eat their food in total silence in order that complete concentration is focused on retraining dysfunctional eating behavior.

PARTICIPANT AS OBSERVER

I entered this setting as a clinical intern. I was also an insider for two reasons. First, I was a practicing psychotherapist for almost three years before coming to California, and I was in the Marriage and Family Therapy Program in the Sociology Department at the University of Southern California. Second, at the time I was in OA and considered myself a recovered overeater with significant weight loss. I spoke the "language" of the recovery program at the SED. I also shared, for the most part, its philosophy.

Concerning the issue of informed consent, the hospital administrator and clinical director of the unit gave me permission to attend and observe the daily events on the ward and at various staff conferences as a clinical intern and as a sociologist with an interest in eating disorders. All the patients were told by the staff that I was "a clinical intern working on getting her Marriage Family and Child Counselor license and gathering data for a paper on eating disorders." I was formally introduced during education groups the first week and informally introduced to any new patients thereafter on an individual basis.

The long-term nature of my internship allowed me to develop relationships among the staff. I observed and talked with them in professional and private settings such as meals, breaks, informal get-togethers, and on occasion, rides home from work.

Treatment Rationale

The staff position is that every patient on SED is suffering from a life-threatening disease that is "cunning, baffling, and powerful." Therefore, any available treatment that is perceived to cause the disease to go into remission is acceptable and attempted with patients. Staff honestly believe that labeling patients as "compulsive overeaters" and utilizing emotion management techniques are essential for recovery. They sincerely believe they are helping patients and do not engage in any therapeutic activity with the intention of hurting them.

Patients, in turn, submit and sometimes appear to embrace assignments and rituals because they want to recover from "this disease." They report feelings of shame, self-disgust, and remorse for their appearance and their behavior. They believe this "rite of passage" leads to recovery. They want desperately to believe it and the overwhelming majority at least say they *do* believe that hospital treatment will "make me better." This is the treatment program of "last resort" for most patients. They want so desperately to fit in and be "normal" that they are a very vulnerable population.

The style of "participant-observation" research let me follow staff very closely. However, because I was also an observer (as a student intern), rather than regular staff, I could maintain a somewhat independent perspective. As Millman states in *The Unkindest Cut* (1977, p. 17) dealing with backstage physician behavior:

> The observer must learn how to enter this "social world" and create her own niche in order to get close enough to the "insiders" to understand how they see their world. Simultaneously, the observer must avoid identifying too much with the "insiders" and their perspectives.

However, I was not in a position where I could freely stand back and remain uninvolved. It was easier for everyone that I acted like one of the staff.

Joining the Staff

By being available to staff and by accompanying them in everyday activities, I observed how they viewed and gave meaning to the situations that arose and how they chose to pay attention to some things and not to others. Because I was present (and "on-call") for five months, I not only observed their behavior, but I also asked staff about their thoughts and feelings as events unfolded. At first, I was able to avoid taking any stand in order to maintain my objectivity. Increasingly this position was untenable, and I participated as a student intern. Also I began to care personally about the staff and patients and I felt some moral obligation to share my opinions. In addition, if I failed to participate I was failing my obligation to the staff in *their* minds. In most cases I maintained a supportive response toward staff policies and procedures. But on occasion I did suggest an alternative to a proposed treatment if I felt strongly that the treatment could be antitherapeutic to the patient.

Every social world has its own rules, rituals, and roles. To be a participant or insider on SED meant that I was guided by this socially shared "definition of reality." However, as an observer, I was not guided by the same rules of attention and interpretation taken for granted by those on the inside. For example, one afternoon I overheard a staff member complaining about the discovery of an anorexic patient exercising in her room. I did not share the counselor's interpretation that this behavior made the patient "a sneaky little bitch."

For the first three weeks, I had the status of observer. Mary (the clinical director) informed me that, "In group [family therapy sessions] we want you to keep silent and just watch for three weeks. After that, you can do co-therapy [participate]." Mary also told me I must not write during any of the clinical therapy sessions because "the patients don't know you and [we] don't want you to write down anything they say...it's confidential."

Although I explained that all my field notes were confidential and as a clinic intern I was highly sensitized and committed to the ethics of confidentiality, Mary stated, "It's policy, Robin. Don't write in the therapy groups." I complied with this request. However, I took profuse notes immediately after the sessions when there was approximately a 15-20 minute break. At the end of each evening the staff elicited my assistance in charting the patients records. The counselors said they were "so overloaded with work, we'd never get out of here without your help." The hospital's administrative policy requires that they remain on the unit until they complete charting the records. Although they do not have to write reports on aftercare patients, they are responsible for writing complete charts on active patients. Because they wanted to go home early they requested my assistance.

During charting, the individual family cases are discussed briefly. For the other counselor's benefit, the entire staff repeat stories of social interations concerning patients. The more humorous, tragic, or dramatic accounts are usually presented in some detail. Immediately upon leaving the clinic, I would go home and reconstruct sessions based on my earlier notes and memory. I also took a thorough set of notes during the second family education session. After the first three weeks, I was more a participant than an observer assuming the role of clinical intern. I was still able to continue my note taking strategies in the second session. However, at times, I didn't have my full 20 minutes for notes after the family therapy sessions because staff expected me to participate in the informal staff gatherings between the sessions. There were occasions when I took notes in the bathroom during breaks in order to record rather than wait for a later time. This also provided greater privacy. I continued assisting staff in charting patient's records throughout my study.

Problem Areas

There were several sources of difficulty in this setting. During the third week of my internship, while Mary was away on vacation, Ellen (counselor) brought to the staffing two requests from people who wanted to volunteer on SED. The staff response was very negative, especially toward volunteers with no OA experience. When Ellen stated that one volunteer was "writing a book about anorexia," the response was hostile.

Maggie: "No way!"
Alice: "Well, we don't want to be used!"
Maggie: "It's very important that we make a stand here."
Alice: "We want people who know what we are about here...no snoops!"

Jody: "What about Mary [clinical director]?"
Ellen: "If we wait for her, she'll say yes to anyone who'd volunteer.

At this point, I felt very uncomfortable. I believed that some of their anger might be indirectly aimed at me because the clinial director "forgot" to consult the staff about my placement on the unit. After heated debate, staff agreed to give a strongly worded statement to the two potential volunteers indicating that they must have OA experience before being admitted as volunteers to the unit. The staff explicitly stated that any volunteers must first attend OA meetings twice a week for a minimum of three months before being permitted on the unit. (To my knowledge, neither "volunteer" contacted staff again.)

Another area of frustration for me concerned eliciting from a particular counselor her interpretation of interactions between patients and staff. Repeatedly, she insisted "But we are all the same, we have the same disease—we all have the same stories...there really aren't any differences," or "We have a universal problem— and, Robin, how can you write about this? Because you are one of us—you can't write about them [patients] and us [therapists]. You have the same disease, the same feelings, the same thinking." This universalizing attitude is documented in the literature by sociologist Marcia Millman who analyzed the intersubjective meaning of body size in organizations such as Overeaters Anonymous. She states, "One of the informal rules of OA is that its members should not judge each other" or "take inventory of anyone else" (Millman 1980, p. 44). According to Millman, OA draws distinctions between members as little as possible and stresses universal problems. Differences are minimized or avoided. Members learn not to argue or disagree with one another.

The unit staff continually stress the universality of the eating disorder patient. In daily practice, however, there was considerable variation in the interaction between staff and patients. Furthermore, staff used informal social labels to distinguish between different types of patients, as I will discuss in the next chapter "Entering the System."

In addition to the ongoing preoccupation with universality and the attempts by the staff to draw me in as a partisan insider, another major concern of mine was the content of my field notes. In my first clinical staff meeting, I was introduced as a "clinical intern who is doing some research on eating disorders." As I began taking notes, one of the paraprofessional counselors commented about my writing to another counselor. "I wonder what she's writing about us?" When I looked up, she was trying to unobtrusively peer over my shoulder at my notes. Sheepishly she said, "You were so busy writing..." She sat back in her chair. I smiled and replied, "I'm new at this, so I'm trying to get it all down and figure it out later. I'm pretty confused." Then she smiled, said "OK," and appeared to relax somewhat.

A few weeks later, I discovered that the staff were preoccupied with determining whether I included their "personal" comments and criticisms of the administration. Over time, they were more comfortable with me and my note taking and made obscene jokes in staffing. They then asked, "Did you get that all down, Robin?" And we would all laugh. Toward the end of my third month on the unit, my note taking behavior elicited no further comments in staffings and it appeared as though most of the staff were no longer concerned with my note taking nor were they apparently censoring sensitive personal material. In comparison to the majority of the staff, a major exception was "Mary," the clinical director. Mary was not only interested in the content of my field notes, she was obsessed with obtaining a copy of "everything you've written." Although the manifest reason for requiring a copy was that she needed to keep informed of my progress, she also had an ulterior motive—she was planning to write a book.

Over the course of my internship, my field notes were a major point of contention with the clinical director. After the first three months, I had several hundred pages of notes. She requested that I give her my notes so that she "could copy them so I could have a set for myself." I discussed this situation with my committee advisor, who suggested delaying confrontation for as long as possible. I accomplished this by meeting for supervision with the clinical social worker instead of Mary.

I was concerned for two reasons. The first involves using my notes as a means of obtaining confidential information from other counselors and patients concerning the clinical director. In some cases, this material was so sensitive I believed it could lead to the firing of one of the counselors and to the detrimental treatment of several of the patients. My second reason was I did not want her to use my notes for her own book.

In the fourth month, the clinical director announced in a staffing that she was:

> Writing a book and planning on using all the stuff you [the counselors] have worked on, with your permission, of course. And I'm also going to copyright everything I've had any input on, because I'm going to take it with me if I leave here...I'm going to thank each one of you personally, in my book, for all those exercises you've written. Is that OK with you?

She then looked around the group and got everyone's enthusiastic nod of approval, except mine. I felt trapped. I said hesitantly, "I guess so, sure." When we left the staffing, she came up to me and stated: "You haven't given me a copy of your notes, Robin. I want to see them." I informed her I was talking to my advisor in the morning and would be willing "to bring them to show you in supervision tomorrow afternoon." Her response was "Good," and I was dismissed. I immediately called my advisor who recommended that I not turn over the notes, but agree to review them with the clinical director. I was also to pull out any extremely sensitive material from my notes prior to meeting with her.

The appointment with the clinical director was set for 2:00 p.m.; however, I was not called into her office until 2:50 p.m. (the staff meeting was at 3:00 p.m.). She apologized, then demanded my notes. I explained that I was willing to review them with her. She insisted, "I don't have time for that, Robin. You give them to me and I'll have them copied and back to you by tomorrow." I told her I was unwilling to do that because of the sensitive material in the files and stated, "I didn't want just anyone to see these notes." She then insisted that the xerox person would be a member of the staff. Again, I refused politely and was dismissed by Mary.

Over the past months, I had made substantial headway toward joining the staff. I was invited to special "get togethers" at the home of staff members and was in the process of obtaining a paid part-time position on the unit. My job responsibilites would include serving as a relief person for staff during emergencies, jury duty, and vacations. Staff and I saw this as a gesture of my acceptance among them as a competent and trusted peer, because each staff member was privately asked her recommendation— which Mary later told me "was unanimous."

Unfortunately, as the news spread on the unit of my refusal to give the clinical director my field notes, tension began to increase. Staff members appeared to be torn between fairness to me and loyalty to the clinial director. This situation escalated over time as the clinical director spoke to me only when necessary and was extremely critical of my work. During the fifth month of my internship, I received an ultimatum from Mary concerning the field notes. This eventually resulted in my terminating the research at SED, after approximately five and a half months on the unit.

Analysis

Although this internship ended abruptly, I had extensive field notes concerning patient-staff interaction. In fact, I accumulated over 800 pages of single-spaced transcripts and field notes. I made three copies of all this information. One copy was stored at the home of a friend for safekeeping. The remaining two I used for coding and for cut and paste work. At this point, the data analysis appeared almost overwhelming as I waded through the material in search of themes, patterns, and trends. However, I found that I could consistently match up statements of staff and patients with my observations and that I was able to compare various sources of information to uncover any inconsistencies thereby increasing the reliability and validity of the research.

After reading my field notes several times, I coded and summarized my notes in the margins. Using colored pens, I then developed a system of indexing, concentrating on the categories of labeling, assignments and rituals, and storytelling. Later, I used the second copy of my notes for cutting and pasting as I put together chapters with the appropriate field notes for the first few (very rough) drafts. I met frequently throughout my internship and afterwards with my committee chair. She gave me support, encouragement, and suggestions for note-taking and recording, analysis, and the theoretical and substantive focus.

Langness and Frank (1985) make the following comments concerning the transformation from raw data into a cohesive, understandable manuscript.

> Generally the subject of a biography has a much more coherent, organized life than people in real life seem to experience. Biographers begin with

the pattern and supplement it with anecdotal material. Otherwise, the random data of which biographical records are composed would overwhelm the reader. The result would be perplexing, and quite possibly unreadable (Langness and Frank 1985, p. 104).

My experience with data analysis was somewhat similar. For example, throughout the internship, I recorded numerous instances of staff labeling patients in the closed staff meetings. These labels were informally used by staff to denote a particular "type" of patient. Staff would also frequently group patients spontaneously, such as "She is just like Angie and Jan." Although the staff could easily recognize and justify the labeling of a patient into a particular patient type, they did not envision a larger interpretive schema. Within this setting, the hospital staff informally classified patients into four kinds of combinations based on two sets of loosely defined variables: resistance to treatment and potential for recovery.

Although I present these four categorial labels in a succint and schematic format, these labels were not, in the majority of cases, discussed in the presence of the patients. For the most part, this informal labeling process was accomplished in closed staff meetings, and information exchanged among staff was considered highly confidential. In addition, the staff frequently used several adjectives and descriptions for each patient. From these multiple descriptions, I compiled the four discreet categories of "good girls," "bitches," "blobs," and "slimeballs/crazy-makers."

The four labels were drawn entirely from the staff statements about patients. Because there were more than four names commonly used by the staff to describe and categorize the patients, the "label" represents a broader concept designed to represent a social typing used to distinguish patients for the staff. Each label represents a distinct type of patient that requires a different treatment approach.

There are some rituals that are universally assigned to every patient in SED. However, while analyzing the labeling process, I noticed that some tasks are predominatly assigned to patients that are labeled a certain type and I call these "individualized" rituals of reformation.

And while studying patient's responses to staff, one theme reoccurred most frequently. This theme was storytelling. I examined the types of stories told and made up the classifications of "tales of the painful past," "horror stories of the unengaged" and "luminary sagas." While the clinical director downplayed the stories as unimportant because she was more interested in what the institution was doing for patients, I was interested in the patient response to the institution and its mechanisms of control.

In the beginning, as I looked for patterns in the labels, rituals, and stories, I found myself focusing on the more punitive aspects of this treatment program. According to anthropologists Langness and Frank (1985, p. 76),

> The ethnographer's entry into the field is always a separation from his world of primary reference—the world through which he obtains, and maintains, his sense of self and his sense of reality. He is suddenly confronted with the possibility of otherness, and his immediate response to this Otherness is to seek both the security of the similar and the distance and objectivity of the dissimilar. He vacillates between an overemphasis on the similar or on the dissimilar; at times, especially under stress, he freezes his relationship with—his understanding of—this Otherness. He may become overly rigid, and his rigidity may determine the "texts" he elicits and the form he gives them.

The first time I analyzed my field notes, the dissimilar" appeared so brutal I could not comprehend why patients stay in treatment on SED. However, after repeatedly reviewing my notes (and having some time elapse in the interim), I began to grasp the perspectives of staff and patients toward the SED treatment rationale and my overly rigid, negative focus began to expand to, hopefully, a more sensitive comprehension of the content and context of staff-patient interactions. Myerhoff (1978) proposed that one undergoes a transformative process in trying to empathize with the reality of others. And I found this personally to be true for me.

Although the selectivity and focus of this ethnography has evolved with each draft, it is still not a comprehensive project. There are subjective meanings and nuances in interpretation which are lost because though I was an insider, I was not "inside" the minds of these patients and staff. Langness and Frank (1985, p. 88) allege that as social scientists "any view we may take is partial; no perspective includes all perspectives" and that "our motives are hidden, even from ourselves."

After analyzing the field notes thoroughly several more times, the substantive focus of my study developed into the social career of "recovering" compulsive overeaters in a clinic that deals with patients who are hospitalized for an eating disorder. The theoretical focus of the ethnography, however, was more elusive. Eventually, after more analysis of the field notes, the theoretical focus evolved into how types of social interaction affect the expression of emotions that are assumed to control eating behavior. From this breakthrough, I drew together the basic themes of the research in terms of entering, working and leaving the SED program, themes that parallel Goffman's and Van Gennep's stages of the transition process.

When patients enter the SED system, several measures are taken to insure that the staff establishes and maintains social control over the patients. The staff take scrupulous precautions to separate the patient from the outside world. They also institute careful preparations for introducing patients to the hospital milieu and the "recovery" process on the unit. In this stage of initial social interaction between staff and patients, staff label patients with various deviance designations and redefine patient's interpretive frameworks in terms of the "disease" model of "compulsive overeating."

Chapter III

Entering the System

During the intake stage, staff typify each patient using several levels of labeling that give each patient a new identity. Formally, staff begin by designating a diagnosis of a mental disorder derived from the DSM-III. The staff then proceed to label patients as to a particular type of eating disorder (Bulimia, Bulimarexia, and Anorexia Nervosa.) However, these official labels are only used for chart documentation and the administration does not encourage staff to use them with the patients.

Informally, staff use typification on an official and unofficial basis to codify and manipulate patients. Officially, each patient is universally classified as a "compulsive overeater" and as "sick." Each is also told she has a problem with food because of her self-centered attitude and behavior. Within the first week of treatment, staff unofficially label a patient "good" or "bad;" this label, in turn, has a direct influence on staff prognosis and treatment. Within this classification, a patient is frequently given an informal label as to a particular "patient type." This informal unofficial classification also colors the staff interpretation of diagnosis and prognosis as well as the treatment plan for each patient. This triple labeling process—DSM-III, the universal patient, and the patient subtype—is the basic framework within which the staff base their perception and social control of their clientele.

The consequence of this labeling is continued pressure on the patient to organize her experience in terms of a disease model in which she is powerless over her illness and thus not responsible for past inappropriate eating behavior. The staff expect each patient to struggle with and overcome her resistance toward being labeled as a "compulsive overeater" with a "progressive and lethal disease" and thus accept organizational control.

OFFICIAL TYPIFICATION

Although the staff account for the eating disorder by means of various documentations in the patient's records, the primary diagnosis given is a "major affective disorder." The most frequently used classifications are "Major Depression" and "Depressive Neurosis." Staff designate these particular diagnoses primarily in order for the patient to receive treatment and to assure appropriate insurance reimbursement. Goffman (1961) indicates, in his observations of the process involved in the formulation of a psychiatric case history, that staff tend to focus on and document more frequently the deficiencies and weaknesses rather than positive aspects of the patient's behavior. In SED, the social history as well as medical and psychiatric accounts are biased toward documenting symptoms that support the claim of a major depressive episode in order to validate admission to an inpatient psychiatric treatment program. Also the chart is used to explain why hospitalization is the only therapeutic alternative for these patients. Staff present the SED as "the endpoint in the unavoidable, self-destruction progression" of these patients.

Case descriptions are brief statements, similar in design to those reported by Warren (1983). For example, one case file began as follows:

> Martha Smith: 26 year old single white female. Weight 195 lbs., 5'6'', elementary school teacher. Chronically depressed, decreased energy, social withdrawal, cries easily, suicidal ideation "I want to die." No prior suicidal attempts. Smokes, complains of back problems, constipation. All family members are compulsive overeaters and father alcoholic. Martha reports some OA experience in the past. Has tried alternative dieting methods to control weight with no success at keeping weight off. Diagnosis: 296.30 Major Depression, Recurrent.

Several of the paraprofessional staff privately discuss among themselves feeling "very annoyed because we just can't call it what it really is—compulsive overeating—because of the insurance companies." But they all agree that staff priority should be directed toward "Helping our patients, we really don't care what they [administration] call it...just so they get in [hospital] so we can help them [patients]." The following discussion, concerning charting and diagnosis, involved Ruth (the hospital administrator) and the staff, speaking during a special staff meeting designed to insure that the patients' charts substantiated insurance claims. This illustrates the negotiation that occurs when OA labels have to be forced to fit the insurance labels.

> Ruth: Only the doctor can put the diagnosis on the chart...You need to have bulimia more [documented] to substantiate the psychiatric diagnosis not just the neurotic depression...have to have the diagnosis addressed in the charting as opposed to just writing "doing better."
>
> Mary: I'd like to put a sticker with a P which means stress "psychiatric" on the outside of the patient's chart. Green Tree Insurance says it will pay for acute treatment only, so you need to JUSTIFY exactly what's going on. C.Y.A....Cover Your Ass—we need to do that. Keep it up...be more concrete.
>
> Lisa (Nurse): Until compulsive overeating is recognized.
>
> Ruth: You should do it on all cases.

On occasion, a staff member would suggest using a less severe diagnosis. But she was always encouraged, if not commanded, by the clinical director and the hospital administrator to use a diagnosis that justified hospitalization. While I was present on the unit, there was never a confrontation on the integrity of this decision. All the staff that I came into contact with complied with the mandate from the administration. In fact, when I brought up the matter at dinnertime, the response was "Oh Robin, don't be stupid...we have to do this...it's the truth...they all have the problems, otherwise they wouldn't need to be here!"

In addition to the psychiatric diagnosis of depression, all of the patients are formally labeled by staff as having a particular type of eating disorder. For example, one chart read "Depressive Neurosis: Bulimia." All of these secondary eating disorder labels concern deviant behavioral patterns and obsession with food. Staff defines three types of eating disorders:

Bulimia: Binge eating where the person is frequently obese.

Bulimarexia: Binge eating followed by purging. The most frequently
used method is vomiting. This individual is usually "normal"
weight.

Anorexia Nervosa: The starving of one's self. This person usually
looks severely emaciated yet still complains of feeling "too fat."

Most of the patients in the SED were thirty or more pounds
overweight, and were therefore, officially labeled bulimic. During
the entire period of my observation on SED, there were only two
women labeled as bulimarexics while five were classified as
anorexics in the treatment program.

While the actual charts and formal position of the staff support
a diagnosis of a mental disorder and various types of eating
disorders, in everyday life on SED the universal label is
"compulsive overeater." On a daily basis the staff spend most of
their time and energy reinforcing their position that all patients
suffer from the same universal problem of compulsive overeating
which therefore justifies universal treatment. Staff repeatedly
informed patients that "We are all the same, no matter what you
call us, we have the same disease of compulsive overeating. We
just may act it out differently."

THE UNIVERSAL CLASSIFICATION OF
COMPULSIVE OVEREATER

Within the SED environment, staff and patients reinforce a culture
centered around the problem of compulsive overeating. Within
this culture each patient develops a perspective toward the self and
her eating behavior and toward her relations with other members
of society. The treatment program is designed around the patient
who is "suffering from serious mental and emotional problems
brought on by compulsive overeating." During admission each
patient is informed that she is a "compulsive overeater" and cannot
control her own life." This typification is seen as a means of
separating the patents and staff from the rest of the hospital and
the world at large. In fact, those who do not have an eating disorder
are labeled "the normies" by the staff. On SED, the only "normies"
were the staff psychiatrist and one of the day-shift nurses. The staff

thereby create a definition of the situation as one of "us" versus "them."

Upon arrival in the unit, the staff present a new patient with the following "FACTS": Eating disorders are a combination of mental obsession and physical addiction. While there are three types of eating disorders (Anorexia Nervosa, Bulimarexia, and Bulimia) defined on SED, they are all identified as variations of the same illness. The clinical director's analogy was "they are like different eruptions of the same volcano." Although most overeaters are overweight and most undereaters are less than the normal weight as designated by insurance charts for height-weight tables, making such distinctions was strongly criticized by the clinical director of the SED, who stated:

> I don't think there is a difference between an overeater, vomiter or an anorexic. I think they all have the same kinds of families and problems of control and triangulation.

In a staff meeting involving what a patient should be told concerning the diagnosis the clinical director informed the staff:

> We need to be careful we say it's the same disease. They need to hear it....The patients try to separate themselves into types. They need to hear it and you must keep it in mind!

Staff also reveal to the patient the doctrine that she is powerless over this disease. The intake counselor gives the following information to every newcomer to the unit:

> It is the same thing as saying to the patient who has tuberculosis "If you love me, you'd stop coughing" as to say to the compulsive overeater "If you love me, you'd stop overeating." It's impossible, you could never do it alone.

What is presented to the newcomer is the disease model, similar to the addiction credo from AA. Eating disorders are perceived by the staff as a combination of physical addiction and mental obsession. What the staff perceive as needed to combat this insidious problem is a total change in a person's psychological processes. This information is presented to a patient at every opportunity. In addition, other patients are encouraged to reinforce the unit's philosophy with newcomers.

Aberrant food consumption habits and food obsession are presented by SED staff as the universal physical manifestations of the disease of compulsive overeating. However, the staff recognize that each patient is likely to have a unique pattern of compulsively overeating or obsessing over food. Eating patterns may include consuming inordinate quantities over brief periods of time; nibbling continuously throughout the day and/or evening; hiding food or hiding from others while eating; devouring large amounts of high calorie food or "junk" food during binges; and terminating an eating binge only after interruption, abdominal pain, sleep, or vomiting. The majority of the patients have attempted to lose weight by one or more of the following methods: fasting, severely restrictive diets, induced vomiting, laxatives; and diuretics. According to a prominent psychiatrist in the field of compulsive overeating (Rader 1980, p. 184):

> the overeater can be one pound overweight or even underweight, as in anorexia nervosa, and still be a compulsive overeater. The illness has nothing to do with weight...the problem is with the control of food.

In addition to the physical addiction to food, compulsive overeating is defined as a disease that includes a psychological obsession with food and body weight. As Marcia Millman (1980, p. 43) notes in the chapter of her book dealing with compulsive overeaters,

> OA delves into some of the psychological syndromes that many overweight individuals experience, particularly paradoxical feelings about personal control that are unrealistically excessive in some ways and markedly diminished in others.

Using the OA philosophy on SED, this obsession is attributed to a basic character flaw that underlies the mental and spiritual part of the disease. The staff encourages the patient to define her weight problem as merely the external symptom of deeper psychological problems. Staff frequently inform each patient she is "self-will run riot." She has "lost the ability to control her own life"—via lack of control when eating. However, staff also assert that she is simultaneously functioning under a faulty assumption that she is in control or should be in control of other people and situations.

The patient is advised by the staff that "this faulty thinking leads to unrealistic pride and unnecessary guilt." Staff is likely to then encourage this individual to ritualistically recite the Serenity Prayer as a reminder of what she can or cannot control:

> God, grant me the serenity to accept the things I cannot change, the courage to change the things I can, and the wisdom to know the difference.

Staff declare that each patient is plagued with innate selfishness. The patient is told that she shares with other compulsive overeaters certain personality traits which she is unlikely to recognize while practicing her disease (actively planning a binge, binging, planning a diet, dieting, ad infinitum). The following personality traits are most frequently attributed to the patients by the staff: poor frustration/anxiety tolerance; emotional liability and sensitivity, magical thinking, masking, isolation, defiance/depression, and perfectionism.

Poor frustration/anxiety tolerance is described by staff as the inability to endure an uncomfortable situation or feeling for any length of time. The staff believe that lack of patience is one of the most common characteristics of the compulsive overeater. During a staff meal, a counselor claimed,

> I hear it all the time in group, they [patients] tell me [therapist] over and over that they can't wait...can't sit on anything. It drives them crazy and then they are bound to eat over it.

Emotional liability and sensitivity pertain to the staff perception that the patients are emotionally volatile and habituated to eating in response to emotional cues. For example, a patient named Karen was not personally invited to the Thanksgiving dinner party on the unit. Her counselor reported that Karen interpreted this oversight as a personal snub. "She told me [counselor] right after lunch, 'I know everybody hates me. I'm starved!' And we had just finished eating! Karen is *so* sensitive!"

Patients' "magical thinking" concerns believing in the unbelievable claim "Eat all you want and never go hungry...just watch the fat melt away...." Many of the patients report that prior to admission to SED they had used a number of diet gadgets promising almost instant relief from fat. The long list included vibrating belts and tables, rollers, rubber suits and "tummy bands," diet pills and diet candy, rubbing creams and diets by the dozens. Mary commented during a staff meeting:

> And then they come in here looking for more magic...they want the easier, softer way...and that's when we have to help them see they have to work at totally changing themselves...

Patients "cover up" their true emotions, according to staff, by blocking or "masking" their negative feelings via the overeating and obsessing over food. Beyond food dependency, overeaters are perceived as excessively emotionally dependent on others even though they appear to be in control. Alice, a staff member, noted during a break between therapy sessions,

> Grace was into being perfect. She dressed "perfect," she talked "perfect," she was a "perfect" lady.... It took her forever to write her First Step, because she couldn't do it perfect—we wouldn't accept it. She'd write what she thought we wanted to hear...not what she was really feeling.

Overeaters are viewed by the staff as insecure loners who have lived very isolated lives. A staff member noted, "In group, they [patients] will share for the first time their deepest feelings. Most of them are loners, even when they have husbands or boyfriends. They don't think anyone could understand the pain they're in."

Another common trait attributed to patients is defiance/depression. The staff state that many of the patients tend to reject others, believing that they would eventually be rejected. "And if they weren't actively hostile, then they were automatically depressed. Because depression is anger turned inward and these are VERY, VERY angry people," remarked the clinical social worker during dinner one evening.

The staff dictum "we strive for progress, not perfection" is commonly heard on the unit. The staff interpret perfectionism as a "script for self-defeat" in that the patients are believed to be absorbed in all-or-nothing thinking in which moderation is a sign of failure and mediocrity. A staff member stated,

Almost everyone here will tell you how one thing, like a dessert at a party, caused her to blow her diet and gain fifty pounds....either you are perfect or you are fat and a failure. They all say the same thing.

The SED staff also include extreme moralistic thinking, manipulation, workaholism, fear of success, fear of intimacy, no realistic self, and ego struggles as personality characteristics contributing to the vicious weight loss and gain cycle.

Counselors receive severe criticism from the clinical director for behavior that does not reinforce the staff philosophy of universality of treatment. On more than one occasion, I witnessed a staff member being reprimanded by the clinical director for behavior seen as "favoritism which could lead to a patient thinking she is special."

> Sandy, you really did wrong....You called me at 7:30 in the morning to talk to me about patients and I thought you wanted to talk to me....Your healthy side wanted to "fess up." But you didn't tell me until now that you stayed after group with Cathy [patient]. And you know that's against the rules. You just want to be a special counselor [Sandy began to cry] you want to be special...we don't want that here. We don't treat patients to individual sessions. That's nonproductive. It was a power maneuver on your part. Your old issues are coming up again. You can't work on it here. [Sandy sobbed violently.] I tell you because it'll hurt you. You get so involved with them and it makes you crazy. You can't do it. It will hurt you and it's not my policy here.

On another occasion Jean (clinical social worker) was admonished by Mary (clinical director) because she gave a psychsocial historical evaluation to a newly admitted airline hostess before she completed evaluations on several other patients. Another stewardess was so upset because it was her "official" turn to be evaluated that she reported it to the clinical director. Mary, in turn, confronted Jean in a staffing:

> Yeah, and Irma got all upset because she hadn't been done and it had been weeks and you took Maureen before her. You know the patients know...can't fool them....I can't have my patients compromised this way. I can see I lose my values when I treat a group like airline hostesses as special and try to promote business. Kissing up to them means it affects patients....I can see how this place is destroying all I've stood for. Slimy, corrupting...permeates all areas.

These incidents support the analysis of trouble in a psychiatric board and care facility by Emerson, Rocheford, and Shaw (1983) which reported that staff project an image opposite to that of an "unpredictable environment full of favoritism." These researchers also note that staff are likely to establish collective definitions of particular patients and the nature of the problems. Then, after examination and evaluation of existing strategies, the staff implement remediate responses. Staff members also use the knowledge gained to disseminate information to the other staff about the patient's life in general. In everyday life on SED, as in the board and care facility studied by Emerson, Rocheford, and Shaw, the informal unofficial patient labels are used by the staff as a means of justifying the specific causes, symptoms, prognosis, and preferred treatment for the patients so labeled.

THE INFORMAL LABELING OF PATIENTS INTO PARTICULAR PATIENT TYPES

In closed staff meetings, staff frequently assign patients various descriptive labels. These labels are unofficially employed to categorize patients based loosely on patients' resistance to treatment and potential for recovery. In order to understand this labeling process, it is necessary to explore both onward interactions and staff ideology and biography. The typification of patients is influenced by the combined expertise, perceptions, and personal values of the staff.

Stimson (1974) examined 19 studies concerning the doctor-patient relationship in which the ideal image of a patient was a passive, obedient, and unquestioning recipient of medical instructions. Stimson (1974, p. 100) notes that,

> It is the doctor who "knows best." Thus the patient is to be passive, obedient and unquestioning. He is not seen as being able to make decisions of consequence regarding his illness or medication or seen as able to evaluate the doctor's actions.

Conversely, patients who have expectations of their physician, evaluate the physician's actions, and/or wish to make their own treatment decisions are viewed by the physician as deviant and therefore "bad" patients. The staff on SED have similar opinions regarding what constitutes a "good" or a "bad" patient.

Resistance to treatment is defined by staff in terms of the labels "good patient" and "bad patient." In order to be labeled a good patient one must demonstrate minimal resistance to the treatment program. This "good" patient, who is dedicated and serious about her recovery, has the following attributes: she attends all therapy sessions on time; always completes "homework" assigned by the staff; and maximally utilizes available services such a nutrition counseling, optional OA/AA meetings, and exercise therapy. A good patient is maximally dependent on the SED treatment program, while maximally independent of others (as individuals) on the unit. One example was a patient named Molly; who was a favorite of several counselors. Sandy, Molly's primary counselor, exclaimed during a break between therapy sessions,

> Oh, she's the greatest! No matter how she feels, she always works [in group]....And she's there for everyone else, too. Did you know she even has two sponsors from OA? One for food and one for the steps!"

In Papper's (1970) article on the undesirable patient, he states that the patient pays a great penalty for not being desirable to the physician. Papper discusses various examples of undesirability, two of which were applicable to several "types" of patients on the eating disorders unit. "Attitudinal undesirability" is most often demonstrated by the ungrateful patient who refuses to deify the physician's expectations and needs. A patient also may be "undesirable on physical" grounds. Patients who are not recovering at the expected rate, or who show a lack of response, and those with a chronic illness fit this category. While Papper noted this type of a patient may be labeled a "crock," similar labelling processes occur on SED when patients are perceived as "bad." In addition, Papper noted that patients who do not respond appropriately to treatment may create frustration and anxiety in the physician who then distances himself from the patient even at a time of greatest need.

The "bad" patient is seen by the staff as inappropriately oppositional to the SED treatment and the OA recovery program. She is in some manner highly critical of the hospital or the therapist and likely to challenge the therapy presented by the staff. A bad patient usually has the following characteristics: she does not attend therapy sessions on time; refuses to do assignments or "did a poor job"; and does not utilize available resources effectively. A bad patient can be actively or passively oppositional to staff. In addition, a bad patient may be either unwilling to leave the unit (having become dependent on a therapist or patient) or overly eager to leave the unit before what the staff consider to be the appropriate time for discharge. Therefore, a bad patient is considered too independent of the SED treatment program and, in some cases, overly dependent on others (as individuals) on the unit.

An example of a bad patient was a woman who refused to turn over her Bible to the staff and was labeled as a "rigid bitch." Within less than two weeks this woman checked herself out of the unit due to an altercation with a staff member who she claimed had insulted her. She was regarded as a "very sick woman" for being so rebellious, despite the staff's finding that her allegation was justified. While staff were relieved that she had left the unit, they also expressed concern for her welfare. They felt she would probably resume her compulsive overeating, and perhaps eventually harm herself in some manner. Interestingly, a staff member also stated, "It's too bad Karen left AMA [against medical advice]. She had great potential, I just know it."

In addition to good patient/bad patient labeling, all of the patients initially are viewed as having some level of potential for recovery from compulsive overeating. A patient's potential for recovery is determined by staff interpretations of the patient's behavior and other background data available to the staff. As Gubrium and Burkholdt (1982, p. 38) note in their study of caregiving in a rehabilitation hospital, "Beliefs and decisions about potential are validated by, and confirm, the staff's approach to the patient in treatment." Once the staff meet the patient, they begin to develop and negotiate an image of the patient based on staff ideology and biography, staff-staff talk, and staff-patient interaction. For example, a patient named Yolanda was readmitted to the unit despite a failure during prior hospitalization at SED. However, the clinical director approved Yolanda's readmission because "she has potential for recovery...I feel she's ready, she seems motivated now."

There are two components to a patient's perceived potential for recovery. The first is the highly ambiguous "readiness" factor. According to staff, "readiness" can overcome even the most severe repeated past failures. Staff define readiness as "when you are prepared to act right away on it...when you are ripe." The second component is the patient's motivation or incentive to change not only her behavior but her total personality. The staff will sometimes recommend a continued stay for a patient, beyond what progress in the past would usually justify, because of "potential." Therefore, once the staff determine the level of potential, this affects the patient's length of treatment.

Once the staff determine that a patient is "good/high potential," an increasingly positive course of interaction follows. In turn, these interactions confirm the staff belief in the patient's potential for recovery. Those patients who are deemed as "bad/high potential" also are likely to receive a significant amount of positive attention from the therapists. The "bad ones" are likely to arouse initial anger and frustration in the staff due to their resistance to treatment, but because of their "high potential" they are seen as appropriate investments for staff time and energy. Patients who are classified as "good/low potential" typically receive a superficial or indifferent response from the staff—both in staff meetings and during actual patient-staff interactions. The fourth type, "bad/low potential" patients, receive the greatest amount of negative or punitive attention from the staff.

Ort, Ford, and Liske (1964, p. 25) in studying the patient-caregiver relationship state that "Evidence from several sources indicates that the attitude of helpers toward client resistance is rather negative." These researchers asserted that the most frequently reported dissatisfaction claimed by physicians stems from lack of control over the patient because of difficult or uncooperative behavior. They also noted that physicians often attribute the break-down of the of the doctor-patient relationship to the patient rather than to the physician's own limitations. In the majority of cases on SED these "bad/low potential" patients are likewise seen as the "most aggravating and time-consuming" of all patients on the unit. Staff invest substantial energy in planning and attempting therapeutic interventions with these patients. Although few of them show remarkable "progress," those who have "personality transformations" become legends on the unit, are subsequently publicly relabeled as "good girls," and eventually receive the laudatory label of "recovered compulsive overeaters." Figure 2 is a schematic representation of the four types of classifications for patients on the SED.

Figure 2.

		Resistance		
		Good Patient	Bad Patient	
	High	* Good Girls	* Bitches	*
		*	*	*
Potential				
	Low	* Blobs	* Slimeballs/	*
		*	* Crazymakers	*

Patients are categorized in terms of resistance and potential in order to assist staff in determining the prognosis and most effective treatment plan for each patient. This informal typification expands into four particular types: good girls; bitches; blobs; and crazymakers/slimeballs. All future staff-patient interactions and therapeutic interventions are to some extent based on these staff-assigned epithets.

Good Girls

The "good girls" are the staff favorites. They are highly motivated, emotionally accessible and willing to work with the staff. They are defined as being "open, honest and willing," and most likely to be perceived as "recovered" at the end of treatment. Leslie Fiedler (1960) proposed that girls are trained to be "seriously" good and to be ashamed of being bad, while boys are overtly encouraged to be good but covertly given suggestions not to be "too" good. In addition, Hochschild (1983, p. 165) denoted the "adaptive, cooperative" woman as "actively working at showing deference," in order to put her own feelings at the service of others. Hochschild (p. 165) further stated that in order to outwardly display a "good girl" demeanor, a woman must also "evoke feelings that make the 'nice' display seem natural."

The classification of good girls on SED includes three subtypes of patients: the *rescuers/superachievers,* the *dolls,* and the *retreads.* The rescuers/superachievers are those patients that develop a style of "not showing any neediness." They are eager helpers and managers of others and rarely give adequate time, space, or energy toward satisfying their own needs.

An extremely obese patient named Veronica was typical rescuer/superachiever. During a meal, Veronica's name was mentioned and Ellen (counselor) remarked:

> That Veronica is something else. She took care of her younger brothers when she was growing up because her parents worked. One of them turned out to be a real bum, but she's still supporting him...and now she's taking care of her parents, raising kids and works full time as a probation officer...and she wants to go get an A.A. degree too!

Patients who receive the subclassification of dolls are believed to be "innocent" or "fragile." If age is a factor, a patient may be labeled a "baby doll." And, if she has an ethnic heritage, the label may be, for example, a "China doll." The staff perceive dolls as more passive than the other types of good girls. However, they are motivated, willing, and usually emotionally accessible to the staff. An example was a youthful looking Asian woman named Lily. Sandy (counselor) whispered to me during an outing with the patients:

> I've been watching Lily and she's been working so hard on her homework. I'm so proud of her....She's so calm and gentle, I really love her....She's just a little China doll....

The final subcategory involves those patients who are returning to the unit for treatment. They are labeled retreads and are seen as possessing high potential for recovery "because" as one staff member proudly asserted "they *know* this is where they need to be and they did something about it! They came back!" The retreads, as well as the other subtypes of good girls, are frequently utilized by the staff as a means of orienting newcomers to the unit because of their high motivation "to get into the recovery program," and their low resistance to therapeutic interventions.

Alice (counselor) was talking with me when a patient named Abby walked by us. Alice called Abby over and requested the following:

> Abby, you are doing so well—and are such a great example of this program—will you go talk to Edith? She's new and has been down this

road so many times she's about lost all hope, and your story will inspire her, I know it....And don't forget to tell her you're a retread, so she can see how far you've come.

Bitches

The "bitches" are the rebels of the unit. They are highly resistant to treatment and yet possess the qualities of readiness, vulnerability, and high motivation. In the unit meetings, these women are usually referred to as "bitches" because of their highly rebellious position toward the staff and treatment program. However, these patients are also an exciting challenge for the staff "because you know if you can just crack that shell that they'll spill their guts and all the pain will pour out and [then] they can get on with it [recovery]." The following account was from a staffing discussing the treatment of one such rebel:

Maggie: The next person is Katy. It's her first week and she is hostile and furious about everything...but she's holding it in and looks like she's going to explode any minute...I guess I'm a little afraid of her, she's so big and mean...My plan was to confront her and there was no time to get to that today. I'll address it next week.

Mary: She rebels against authority figures.

Dr. C: She puts her anger all over the place and puts off her own confrontation [of her illness].

Mary: She is no longer compliant. Katy is aggressive. Have you interpreted this for her?

Maggie: Yes.

Mary: Good. Don't let her into group unless she says she wants in.

Dr. C: I don't think she should be punished. I see you're angry. But what is the big thing you are angry about?

Maggie, Mary, and Lisa: We all are saying that.

Maggie: She's real hostile, but even when confronted, she has refused to let it blow off [express more openly her anger].

Jody: Point out to her that she has created this as part of her style...Countrywide Airlines are investing in her [recovery].

Lisa: You can't ignore her, you have to confront her and it will all come out because she's ready to work on it now [her negative emotions]. [Several of the staff nodded.]

Maggie: I agree.

Blobs

These patients are quiet, "good" and never cause any problems around the unit. They keep up with homework assignments and any assigned tasks. However, they make very little impact on the staff or their fellow patients because their "work" is usually defined as "mediocre at best...so bland." They are perceived as having very low potential for recovery due primarily to low vulnerability and low motivation. Staff discussed one "blob" in a meeting devoted to negotiating her discharge summary:

> Maggie: She's so boring and bland.
> Ellen: Disgusting.
> Maggie: No. She's not. Just bland. My goal for her is to be more in touch with her feelings. Maybe in aftercare [she'll improve]...she's a very superficial person.
> Ellen: She's a very lonely person. Maybe we can discharge her now.
> Mary: Do you think she's gotten the OA concepts you want her to get?
> Maggie: Well, she's so wish-washy. It's like erosion—it takes time.
> Jody: Doesn't mean she's a failure. But she's gotten all that she's to get now.

Blobs receive many names from the staff to describe their incompetent, weak performance. Staff label patients as "victim," "wet noodle," "dead," "wimp," "pussy," "soft," "benign," "wishy-washy," "space cadet," "whiner," "people-pleaser," "kiss-ass," "passive sickie," "gag city," and "emotional runaway."

Whereas unofficial staff labeling is generally restricted to staff, the "blobs" are an exception. Perhaps because these patients are the least threatening to the staff, they are frequently told outright the label they have been given by the staff. Janice, for example, was overtly labeled a "BLOB" because she was perceived as being very passive and unemotional, having low motivation to change, and because she was very extremely obese and very plain. Although Janice was very "good" when it came to writing her assignments and habits of cleanliness, she was "bad" because she "got on Alice's [therapist] nerves" during group therapy and Alice told her "to shut up because you are talking too much and not saying anything." Janice very often "whined" to her peers and in group therapy that the labeling she had received was arbitrary and prejudiced against her. However, she felt she was powerless to change it because she was easily intimidated by the staff and other patients. One afternoon, she told me bitterly, "I've been typecast a blob, and I know it. I hate it but I can't do anything to change their thinking...." Indeed, this label was very difficult to change because in addition to her "bland, dull" behavior and "inanimate, moronic" personality, Janice has a speech defect that makes her speech slow and somewhat unclear.

Although staff occasionally acknowledge that patient behavior is somewhat situational, role specific, and relational, they persist in using the labels they have assigned during the initial staffing, fitting all subsequent behavior into the category they have chosen for the patient. However, it the patient's behavior changes very drastically, then a new label will be negotiated by staff. Such a negotiation occured with Janice three weeks later during a family group therapy session.

Over time, Janice had become more and more upset by this label. Finally, she decided to confront Alice on this issue in the family session. However, Janice became hysterical and broke down into such deep sobbing that she was unable to continue speaking for several minutes. The therapist chose to reformulate Janice's emotional outburst as progress. Alice said, "You are becoming more real and genuine with your feelings....I think you are learning to stand up for yourself, and set some limits as to what you'll take from others." The therapist then informed the other patients in the group that "this is a healthy and normal response....Janice is working now...she's getting into her recovery....Janice is becoming a good girl, now."

Slimeballs/Crazymakers

The *slimeballs* and *crazymakers* are the polar opposites of the "good girls." Slimeballs and crazymakers are the anathemas of the unit. Staff consider these patients to be poorly motivated, emotionally inaccessible, and highly resistant to any therapeutic interventions attempted by the staff. This classification is divided into two types based on whether or not the staff perceive the patient's actions as deliberately manipulative or truly pathological.

Slimeballs are presumed to be covert troublemakers and their behavior is interpreted as always involving passive hostility toward treatment. The majority are described as "slimy," "sneaky," or "slippery" because when staff confront them on "their bullshit," these patients deftly avoid responsibility by using denial and blaming others. They are perceived as highly manipulative.

A patient named Diane, for example, had been in the hospital for twenty-four days and was only covered by insurance for up to thirty days. The staff, therefore, began making plans for her termination. The therapists primary complaint was that this woman, an emaciated anorexic, is "a real slimeball...one of the slimiest, sickest broads on the unit." Here is the account of the staff meeting concerning Diane:

Sandy: ...on the fourth, she goes to fifty percent insurance coverage. Do we tell her?

Mary: No, some are here on fifty percent. We need to get her angry. Push her. She whines and complains, but when we confront her, she's so slippery....She's a real slimeball. She gets everyone else to do her work for her, and then she sits back and says "Yes, but that won't work for me." And comes up with a million excuses!

Sandy: We want to deny her free day! [Patient earned privilege of leaving hospital for several hours unsupervised, usually proceeding the official termination. Deemed by the staff as a "practice for living exercise."] Yes.

Ellen: [Mimicked Diane's manner for the staff. Laughter.]

Sandy: She's been here twenty-four days.

Mary: Dave [Diane's husband] wants her out in thirty days. He says he really wants a lay from her as soon as possible.

Dr. C: She has a hard time making decisions. What her husband, therapist, and peers would say goes through her mind. I try to have her focus on making decisions. See what she thinks then hold onto it.

Mary: She has another side that's real sneaky. She gets nurses to give her husband pills...she's very sneaky on the unit.

Dr. C: She hesitates to express her feelings on everything.

Jody: Maybe we can give her five minutes of time for her to talk about herself in group...lower our expectations.

Mary: She really needs long-term family therapy. We need to identify the aftercare program for them [Dave and Diane], so she can deal with her discharge.

Dr. C: She says she wants to get into an assertion group when she gets out.

Mary: I think she's got you as a big daddy. There's assertiveness here, but she doesn't ask for it.

Sandy: I want her to get her needs met. Maybe we should let her have a pass—so she can get laid and maybe relax.

Dr. C: She reads the staff as rejecting and beating her like her mother. Maybe the staff needs to make it less personal.

Jody: She's obviously a long-term case.

Mary: Why don't you make up a long-term discharge plan for them [Dave and Diane] with specific goals when she leaves on pass this Sunday? [All agree.]

The crazymakers are perceived as *not* having the capacity to recover because they are "unable to be honest with themselves or others...they are just too sick." The crazymakers' behavior and thinking are usually attributed to mental illness. Staff describe them as "really fucked up," "a hard one," "paranoid," "suicidal," "mind-fucker" and "crazy." Frequently, intake information from the social history is used as evidence to support the claim that a patient is a crazymaker. Historical events including accounts of prior psychiatric hospitalizations, suicidal attempts, nervous breakdowns, and bizarre behaviors, are used by the staff to reinforce their position toward these patients. The excerpt that follows was from a staff meeting concerning Wendy, a patient informally labeled as a crazymaker:

Sandy: Wendy has been here eight days. She wrote a first step like a horror story...she's alcoholic and been into drugs and has been in a mental hospital....she needs to be in touch with her feelings.

Mary: How old is Wendy?

Jean: Twenty-three. The worst is when she jabbed her breasts with tweezers to pull out the fatty tissue...she's got scars to prove it. She enjoys the role of crazy. Rose [another patient] became hysterical when Wendy shared, she said Wendy was like her mom and dad in that they couldn't help how sick they were but they were so messed up and it affected her [Rose's] whole life.

Mary: Point out to Wendy, "This is how I chose to live." Don't drive for emotion. She's used to that from her parents and its her defense against emotions...When she says she wants to work—say "No you don't." Now help her accept that's the way she is.

Sandy: I had her write about being a little girl during her inventory...she stopped and said she wanted to laugh...she's just so sick....

Jean: She's honest at least, not like Diane.

On a few occasions, a counselor becomes so frustrated with this type of patient that despite encouragement from the clinical director and the the psychiatrist she informally labels the patient as "hopeless." At this point, if the professional staff feels that the patient deserves "another chance to recover" they usually support the patient while maintaining rapport with the paraprofessional staff member. Frequently, the psychiatrist attributes the problem to past psychological trauma in the patient in order to appease the counselor. If, however, the professional staff feel the patient is truly hopeless, or too great a problem, there is a high possibility of referral to another unit or institution.

During my internship, there were only two occasions when this situation arose. One patient was transferred to the alcoholic unit for detoxification. Another patient was referred to a private mental hospital because "we couldn't handle her here—she was out of control and actively suicidal." Sometimes the director and the administration encourage the staff to keep working with a patient for economic and appearance reasons. "We don't want to lose any we don't have to...and besides, it makes us look bad if we lose too many. So be careful."

The informal labeling of patients into particular patient types has a direct influence on staff interpretation of diagnosis and prognosis as well as the treatment plan for each patient. The informal labeling process, in addition to the universal classification of "compulsive overeater," applies continuous pressure on the patient to accept and embrace her new identity as a compulsive overeater with a "progressive and potentially lethal disease." In response, the patient is expected to recover from compulsive overeating. She must conform at the ideological level by shifting her personal interpretation of her eating and by taking on the proposed identity of the compulsive overeater and at the behavioral level by obeying staff instructions. The staff expect this process to provoke emotional distress; the staff see their role as helping each patient to struggle with and overcome her resistance to the sick label.

THE PATIENT'S STRUGGLE WITH THE COMPULSIVE OVEREATER LABEL

Prior to hospitalization patients explain and justify eating patterns in various ways. Incoming patients often report overeating because they "love the taste of food." They do *not* perceive themselves as sick or incurable. They readily admit having a problem controlling food consumption, however, their analyses of this problem vary. Several patients associate consuming large quantities with the satisfaction they receive from tasting the flavors in certain foods. For example, a patient told me the following account during her first day on the SED unit:

> I went to the dentist to have a cavity filled. He gave me a shot in my mouth and when I went home, I planned to binge. I couldn't taste anything in my mouth! So I spit it out. I really didn't want to eat anything after that...I got no enjoyment from the food because I couldn't taste it. It was too weird.

Another new patient explained that her overeating was directly dependent on the food she ate:

> Taste has a big thing to do with it. I like sharp, strong tastes. I don't overdo it with mild flavors like a green banana that has no taste to it....It has to taste good to me. If it tastes good, I want more of a good thing. I like lots of salt, garlic, hot sauce, and spices!...and I'm sad when it's all finished, cause I wanted more....

Some interpret overeating as a hereditary phenomenon—a physical predisposition traceable to the genetic make-up of their parents. "I eat because it's heredity. Everyone in my family was large or 'big-boned' as we called it. We needed to eat because we were big to begin with." Others relate eating to culture and family lifestyle. "It's ethnic. In my family [Italian-American], all we ate was the heavy pasta that mama cooked. And everyone ate and enjoyed it." Others justify overeating as a response to external events that usually involve uncomfortable relationships or circumstances. "Well, once in a while, I eat because I am frustrated or bored....I come home from work and it's been a bad day and I eat then for satisfaction."

Some patients insist that their problem is purely a physical malfunction of their thyroid gland or a metabolism dysfunction. They firmly maintain that their condition is entirely physical and can be controlled with proper medication. They blame the medical establishment for inept or inadequate treatment. Others believe their overeating is directly related to bad habits they have developed. They view habits, rather than "emotional problems," as the cause or consequence of their behavior. For example, one woman stated:

Well, you see the problem is that I don't eat properly. I skip breakfast because I'm not very hungry in the morning. So late at night, well, I eat to much. All I need to do is get rid of this one bad habit, and then I'll be skinny again.

Finally, patients commonly report overeating as a response to uncomfortable or unidentified emotions. The following are several examples of comments patients made to explain their compulsive overeating habits: "Because I'm anxious about something. I feel afraid and food calms me down"; "When I get worn out or tired, food gives me strength"; "Sometimes I'd have a big project to do and I'd get all ready and then I'd decide I needed some food for energy. And then I'd be eating...I would procrastinate by eating rather than getting started. I guess I feared success or failure...hell, I don't know"; and "I'd eat a lot of the time because I was afraid I'd go hungry later."

While newcomers readily share their interpretive frameworks with the staff, staff resoundingly respond that all alternative frameworks explaining overeating are faulty and in fact extremely dangerous to the patient's welfare. They explain to each patient the importance of recognizing her denial of "this progressively lethal disease over which you are completely powerless."

> No matter what you [patients] say, you are here because you are totally powerless. You don't need an excuse. It's really not your fault....You have to eat—you have no choice. And unless you accept that you can't do it yourself, it'll [disease] kill you.

According to staff in SED, all of the patients are likely to come into the hospital "in denial." Denial to the staff represents a strategic response by the patient to cope with the current reality of being out of control in terms of illness and disease. Disease implies an element of compulsion—overeating is seen as beyond volitional control. Sometimes, the patient reported her own perceptions of her eating as "unconscious." "It's automatic. As soon as I start to watch TV, I turn into an automatic eating machine. It's like I go unconscious, and then next thing I know I've finished the whole thing." Thus, the SED patient is not morally responsible for her overeating and is entitled as a "sick" person to medical and institutional care. Denial, to staff, means ignoring and avoiding the basic premise of the medical treatment program they espouse. This premise is the First Step of the Overeaters Anonymous program: "We admitted we were powerless over food—that our lives had become unmanageable."

The typical newly admitted patient strenuously objects to the label of compulsive overeater because it implies a lack of control, and a sickness model, unacceptable to her self-image. Frequently, she insists that she would rather be labeled as "weak-willed" or "a glutton" and still be considered responsible for her own behavior than assume the staff perspective of an unwilling victim of a "cunning, baffling and powerful disease."

> Let me tell you, I'm tired of being told I have a DISEASE. I mean, really, this sucks. I'd rather you call me a "pig" or a "glutton" or something....I know I eat too much. That's the whole problem. I just want to get a handle on it, and I'll be fine...like, some encouragement would be nice, ya know? This disease stuff really gets me down.

In addition to the moral connotation of the overeater as a victim, there is another implicit assumption involved in this labeling process. Accepting the label of compulsive overeater is an admission of deviance; a way of agreeing with the labelers. When each patient publicly acknowledges in therapy session, "I am a compulsive overeater and I am powerless over my disease," she also implicitly states "And I am not bad because I am sick, but my compulsive overeating is bad." Because overeating is considered deviant in our society, and because the staff define overeaters as "sick," the patient has to change her identity in order to be accepted and proceed toward her recovery. Even in circumstances where the patient denies she has a disease, awareness of that label and her incarceration (however brief) may change her roles, her self-image and her relationships with significant others both inside and outside of this setting.

Such was the situation for Elaine, who left the hospital after only four days because: "I can't stand the problems this is creating. When my husband comes to family sessions, he's told he's a co-addict and he's furious. So I have to leave...my marriage is at stake." Staff members tried "to reason" with Elaine and her husband but they left treatment despite staff promises of her recovery from compulsive overeating.

Compulsive overeating is interpreted as action taken to anesthetize the pain of feelings. Food is presented as a form of self-medication that has become ineffective in the long-term career of the compulsive overeater. This theory permits the patient to integrate past binges and painful experiences into a form of ineffective self-help, as well as reinterpret the moral judgements made about these actions of the past. So the label of compulsive overeater serves to explain and justify feelings and behavior by distributing responsibility to outside the conscious control of the patient. It also provides a means of creating a new identity for the patient.

Given this new framework, the patient then begins to incorporate information to support and maintain her new identity. She begins to reassess the past and current events within the new framework. Her biography is likely to be reconstructed to include a bad, old self and the rebirth of a new, recovered self. As this framework is adopted by the patient, a trajectory of recovery from compulsive overeating develops, permeating her identity in every context of her life.

The labeling process initiated by the staff is reinforced by peer pressure to conform to unit norms. Her audience is thus expanded to include other patients and those family members who have also accepted and embraced this label. Over time, it is increasingly likely for the patient to begin to assume the identity of a compulsive overeater. The label effectively organizes her experiences while reducing guilt and shame, but also the effect of having an extended audience support the compulsive overeater label makes the personal choice of assuming this new label a more attractive alternative than her previous interpretive framework.

Thus, the label of compulsive overeater serves several functions for the SED patient. It reframes "shameful" past eating behavior into experiences beyond her conscious control and therefore absolves her of guilt and shame. It explains painful past negative emotions like frustration and resentment as "too overwhelming" for her to handle without the aid of food as medication. And, it justifies hospitalization because she cannot apparently recover on her own from this disease.

By successfully incorporating the medical interpretation of her conduct and the label it generates, the patient begins the process of replacing her "weak-willed" or morally bad identity with that of the disease identity. Paradoxically, according to the hospital staff, this acceptance will eventually lead to recovering a normal lifestyle.

Chapter IV

Working the Program

Once the patient is labeled and begins to demonstrate acceptance of her identity (Stage 2), the process of "recovery" or "getting better" commences. During this stage the staff is concerned with the patient displaying a "recovering" identity. The staff base their perception of recovering on a patient participating successfully in "working her program." This process is composed of an increasing awareness of her condition, dependency on "appropriate" sources and, finally, action taken to control the expression of emotions which affect her eating behavior. Mary commented to another staff member:

> Elaine has really been working hard this past week. I've seen remarkable progress, she's really turning things over [to her Higher Power] and learning new values. She may get a divorce when she gets out [of the hospital] but it'll be worth it...she'll be sane again.

A patient successfully engaging in self-work is seen as actively pursuing a total personality transformation. This transformational process is determined by staff to be essential for recovery. To recover from dysfunctional eating a patient is expected to "hit bottom" and experience a somewhat linear pattern of improvement. Once transformation is assumed to be undertaken, and staff identity the patient as "into her recovery," she is required to maintain eternal vigilance to prevent a relapse into her illness. For example, after talking with a patient about the recovery process for several minutes, a staff member declared:

75

> You really have to be open, honest and willing to work this program with all your heart in order to get it [recovery]. That's the H-O-W in "How it works." And when you get it [recovery] there will be no stopping you. But you have to stay on guard. You have to stay in fit spiritual condition.

REQUIREMENTS FOR WORKING THE PROGRAM

Throughout "getting better" or Stage 2, the patient is typified as "recovering" or "not recovering." In order to be perceived as displaying a "recovering" identity, a patient must constantly and successfully demonstrate behavioral and ideological conformity. Compliance to program norms is perceived as working a program of recovery.

Because the SED staff define the origin of compulsive overeating as intrapsychic, the primary source of the problem is understood to be the patient's own emotional problems rather than social or familial forces. Thus, the SED staff utilize a therapeutic position that simultaneously blames the disease and the patient for the particular circumstances. Ferraro (1983, p. 305), in a study of survivors in a battered women's shelter, noted:

> The contextual, situational and political nature of defining people's troubles from a therapeutic framework has been ignored. By adhering to therapeutic ideology, staff...focused almost exclusively on emotional problems of individual women.

Similarly, the SED therapeutic ideology attributes primary responsibility for recovery to the patient. Because primary responsibility is placed on the patient, she is continuously evaluated on her personal commitment to engage in "self-work." Staff also refer to self-work as "working the program." As one staff member noted, "Basically, your problems are of your own making and we're here to help you see this and accept who you really are...a compulsive overeater who cannot manage her own life!"

There are three elements for working the program successfully. First, the patient must demonstrate, by increased self-stigmatization, acceptance of the identity of a recovering compulsive overeater. Second, the patient is required to display appropriate dependence. Third, the patient must learn effective emotion management. Staff use terms such as "sincerity" and "vulnerability" to assess qualitatively appropriate self-work.

Increased Self-Stigmatization

As the process of stigmatization continues on SED, and the audience of staff and peers responds to the patient as having experienced an identity change, what follows appears to be a paradoxical reversal. Once the patient accepts the label of compulsive overeater (self-stigmatization), she is perceived as beginning the process of recovery. In order to be seen as "getting better," she has to first embrace the role of being "sick." The following staff position was declared during an education seminar for the patients and their families:

> There is no way for you to recover until you can admit you have a disease that will kill you....It's food that controls you and your behavior—you are defenseless....You can't control it, and if left unchecked, it can be fatal. When you admit powerlessness over food—you are on the road to recovery. That's the point where you begin to get better...that's the starting point. You have to be demoralized—or you'll never get there....And you have to keep admitting it—or you'll lose it [your recovery].

Thus, the staff goal is to universalize the patient's identity by the constant encouragement of this self-stigmatization process. In addition, by stigmatizing the patient, the staff attempt to universalize the patient in terms of her relationship to others on the unit. During a group therapy session, the director told the patients:

> We all have the *same* problem. Everyone in this room knows exactly where you are coming from...Why? Because each of us has been there. And I want you to remember this, it comes from AA but it fits, "No case is hopeless, not even yours." Remember that. We are all the same and you aren't special. You are one of us.

One means staff employ to facilitate a patient's increased awareness of her condition and acceptance of the disease model is the First Step assignment. The First Step is based on the Twelve Step Recovery Program of Overeaters Anonymous. It states:

> We admitted we were powerless over food, and that out lives had become unmanageable.

In the First Step assignment, the patient is asked to publicly admit and accept her powerlessness over food and other people. Staff suggest that she "learn to let go and stop managing the affairs of others." Therefore, as the patient continues to demonstrate increasing awareness of her sick condition, she is perceived to be displaying a "recovering" identity. Stephanie's counselor commented to me in the chart room that night that:

> Stephanie gave her First Step today. She cried through the whole thing. It was so hard for her to admit she's powerless, and needs her Higher Power...she said she felt so ashamed. But I told her that was good and she's really accepting who she really is.

Appropriate Dependency

While the first component of working her program consists of increased self-stigmatization which includes acknowledging primary responsibility for her self-work, the second component involves the "acceptance of assistance from a power greater than herself" (dependency). At this point in treatment, the patient is introduced to the Second and Third Steps of the OA program. The Second Step states, "Came to believe that a Power greater than ourselves could restore us to sanity." While the Third Step is, "Made a decision to turn our will and our lives over to the care of God as we understood Him."

According to the staff these steps do not require that the patient adopt a new concept of God, or even that she believe in God, per se, at all. "Your Higher Power can be nature, the rhythm of the universe, the OA group itself, or a more traditional concept of God." As long as one realizes that there is *something* greater than the self, then the patient is perceived as making a good start. A staff member announced the following information during our dinner conversation:

> We talked about our Higher Power today [in group]. Some of them are so straight and narrow about God...and some are really wild. Wendy's H.P. is the lamp in the lounge. She said, "It's always there, I can count on it." Like it was her best friend! And Cindi has H.P. that's a little magic fairy. It sits on her shoulder and gives her permission to have fun....I like Cindi's best, I think.

What is of paramount importance to the staff is that the patient surrenders her "will" to a force beyond or larger than herself and acknowledges that she is not in control. On occasion, a staff member even suggests to the patient "that the staff itself could be [successfully viewed as] one's Higher Power."

I overheard the following conversation between two patients and a staff member after an in-house meeting of Overeaters Anonymous.

Lucy: I just don't get it, I guess.

Alice
[Staff]: What?

Lucy: What I'm supposed to "turn over" and what I'm supposed to handle myself.

Chris: Do you have a "Higher Power?"

Lucy: Well, yes. I believe in God.

Chris: Well, when I came in here, I didn't. I thought it was all a bunch of bullshit...but I learned that I had to be honest with myself and admit I needed help to get better. So I made the group my "Higher Power"—cause they've got what I want!

Alice: Yes, Chris, that's important. But what Lucy wants to know is— what all does she have to "turn over." Right? [Looks at Lucy.]

Lucy: Yes.

Chris: Everything! You have to turn everything over to your Higher Power.

Alice: Yes, that's right. But you also have to do the foot-work....Remember, "faith without works is dead."

Two key issues develop from this concept of necessary surrender to a power greater than one's self. First, a patient must surrender her individuality to the collectivity of the unit, at least on some overt level. And second, of prime concern to the staff is that the patient learn to distinguish what she can control and can not control. The staff teach that although it is painful to give up such innate qualities as selfishness, desire for control, and hope in "magical thinking," the patient will gain the benefits of recovery only by making "those renunciations and accepting direction from your Higher Power."

During an educational session with patients and family members, the therapist giving the lecture claimed,

The Second Step introduces us to the idea of a power beyond ourselves; a Higher Power we can trust to restore our emotional balance so that we can realize our full potential for good. The Third Step helps us by asking that we place our *will*—our thoughts and feelings, and our *lives*— our actions, in the hands of this Higher Power....We receive assurance that *we are cared for and loved,* and we are encouraged to live as our Higher Power would have us live, rather than as we have lived for so long....

While staff promote the acceptance of assistance from a Power greater than the patient herself, other forms of dependency are severely monitored by the staff. The patient is indoctrinated to depend fully on "the program"—not to depend on staff or fellow-patients for support and guidance. In fact, the director of the clinical program repeatedly chastised one of the paraprofessional counselors. "I don't want them to bring their issues to you....I want them to bring them to group. No private counseling, do you understand?"

The staff also discourage patients from establishing dependency on another patient, friend, or family member. An example of such discouragement occurred during a family therapy session involving a patient named Mary Jo and her husband, David.

Mary Jo: People tell me I look good but I feel awful....I don't know what to do—sometimes I want to talk and sometimes I don't. I feel crazy and I want David to answer and tell me what to do.

Maggie: [to David] And that hooks you in as "CO" [co-compulsive overeater] for her.

David: Yes, she did it and I told her what to do and then I thought "Why did I do that?"

Maggie: Well, it's because you don't want to stand around and watch her be self-destructive. But it's a setup to make you her Higher Power and then after a while you won't have all the answers, and she'll resent you and start eating...

The patient is likewise conditioned not to depend on herself. "You are your own worst enemy" is a phrase repeatedly preached to the newcomer. This experience leaves the patient with a lack of faith in her own ability to judge her behavior, feelings and values. Frequently, this leads to the patient having extreme ambivalence around the issue of termination of treatment. Many reported feeling ill-prepared to reenter the "real world...without my defenses, I feel very vulnerable."

In contrast, the staff actively support and encourage dependency on the SED aftercare program and the OA program and its sponsors. Therefore, for staff to perceive a patient as "being into her program and getting on with her recovery," a patient must be maximally independent of others, as individuals, while involved and dependent on the hospital program and the OA recovery program.

An aftercare patient, named Mary Lou, discussed her adjustment to life outside the hospital during group therapy.

Mary Lou:	I have a new God. He is loving but I don't know why I was so stupid before...I'm fifty years old, and it's about time I learned something quick...[Several participants responded to Mary Lou's statement. The consensus was that she was experiencing a "flight into health."]
Sandy [counselor]:	It takes time—you've had that old God for years.
Bill [spouse]:	I had a crisis last week when my kid wrecked the car and I went crazy and that old God came back...He went away, but He comes in a crisis....
Laura:	It's really hard to live outside and work the program. I know...and I'm almost finished aftercare, and sometime I don't want to leave [SED]....
Sandy:	It was so easy in here to do assignments because it was so structured....but it's the real world out there....I don't write [inventory] every night...I don't call just to chat. I call when I need help, Mary Lou. And I'm lucky because most of my friends are in program [OA] so I can call anytime to get help....It's better to get in the habit of calling, so that you have friends when you need to call—it's hard at first, but you just do it....Call three people a day, no matter what...You do what your [OA] sponsor tells you to do. You do it!

Numerous stories are told of persons who made good progress while in the hospital but who regressed after discharge because they "rearranged their priorities" and treated their (OA) recovery program as unimportant. Each patient and her family are repeatedly warned about this by staff. Even a patient who sees herself as totally independent of others is taught to think of herself as dependent on OA. A typical example was taken from a staff member's comments during group therapy:

I want to warn you, about leaving here and not maintaining your program. If you walk out of here and forget all you learned, and never use the Steps, you are bound to gain it all back and more....I've seen it happen over and over....In fact, look at our retreats in here. They'll all tell you why it happened to them. And they had to come back in again....You have to keep going to OA meetings and working your program, because overeating can be controlled but never cured. You have to keep working your program or you'll only have three choices: to die, to go insane, or to come back and start again...that's so painful....This is just to let you know you don't have to go back there...to hit bottom again.

During treatment, staff continually assess a patient's degree of dependence. Some patients are seen as having various degrees of independence but are "susceptible" to the often well-meant but "harmful" efforts of family members to assist them. Usually it is the "good girls" and "bitches" that follow this pattern.

Chris: And I can't live with my parents because they are CO's too and they'd do the best they could but they don't know recovery.
Terri: They love you Chris, so they'd watch you like a hawk. You'd be a little girl again—dependent on them....
Chris: I know. It's the truth. I'll call them tonight and explain I'm not coming home.

Sometimes, blobs or crazymakers are cast as pathologically "dependent types." One "manipulative crazymaker" was an aftercare patient named Denise. The following interaction occurred during family therapy sessions:

[Denise begins by telling the group about buying zucchini bread for her husband's and son's snacks.]
Joey [son]: We didn't want it anyway, Mom.
Jim [husband]: Wait Denise. You bought it and then told us it was for us when we *told* you we didn't want it.
Denise: But it's nutritious and good...
Maggie [counselor]: What do you really want to tell them?
Denise: That I love them and it bothers me because I've been having a hard time with my food....
Maggie: What do you want to say, Denise?
Denise: That I'm sorry but it's getting harder for me more and more.
Maggie: Yeah, Denise. Let's cut through all this. What do you want to tell them?
Denise: Well, that it bothers me to have to cut the zucchini bread and feel it in my hand.

Maggie: NO! A direct statement. That you don't want the zucchini bread in the house!
Denise: Well, I'm sorry but I'd rather...
Maggie: No. Direct, Denise.
Denise: I've been trying so hard lately, and yet I want to eat....
Maggie: Stop it, Denise. Right now.
Denise: I don't know what you want me to say.
Maggie: What's the bottom line, Denise? What do you want to *say*?!
Denise: I don't know. I don't want to hurt anyone's feelings....
Maggie: You'll have to trust me, Denise. Tell them directly—your feelings.
Denise: Well [pause], well...
Jim: All right, tell me! I mean it, Denise, it's OK.
Denise: Do you really mean it, Jim?
Jim: ...I'd love to hear you say it! Honestly, tell me what you feel. If you are angry—say it!
Denise: OK, I will. I don't like it and I won't buy it for you!
Maggie: Finally. And you had to get his permission.
Denise: I feel so good now.
Maggie: Of course you do. You got his permission to be angry. He's like your Higher Power. And I'm really worried about you, Denise.

In addition to staff concern over dependency toward other individuals, some of the staff also fear that hospitalization itself may unintentionally reinforce dependency. In this setting all meals are prepared for low-calorie, low-carbohydrate, and low-fat consumption. Meal times, as well as the format for eating behavior, are highly regulated. The program also has a tightly structured regime from wake-up at 7 a.m. until bedtime at 11:30 p.m. In rare instances, a staff member may recommend discharge because a patient appears to be overly dependent on the hospital regime.

Emotion Management

The third component of working the program involves the presumed relief of emotions such as guilt, resentment, and fear by actions taken in the form of confession and amends towards others. Staff define and encourage the "appropriate" expression of those emotions presumed to control eating behavior. The purpose of appropriate emotion management is to change the way emotions are expressed in order to eliminate dysfunctional eating. The clinical director addressed the patients and family members about this one evening:

Sharing and making amends are essential tools for personal growth. We can begin to grow with the courage to look at ourselves as we really are. Many of us have been so obsessed with our compulsive overeating that we have little sense of self. We may have lost sight of our personal goals, not reached our potential, or become too concerned with trying to change someone else. Often, our basic good qualities have been hidden by fears and frustration....We want to help you learn how to express your feelings so you won't eat. You used to eat away the anger and pain...we'll teach you how to manage your feelings so you won't have to eat over them anymore.

In daily life, there is considerable practicing of emotional management between staff and patients. Patients are encouraged to be honest and "to deal" with each other, their families, and the counselors in an assertive manners. In fact, unwillingness to confront others (or to be confronted) with personal issues and feelings is seen as resistance to treatment. The following discussion involved several aftercare patients and a counselor during a group therapy session.

Mia: I want to quit my job and move back with my parents next week...it's too rough at work. My boss doesn't like me to use the phone to call my [begins crying] sponsor...

Sandy: You can get through this if you are honest...Tell your boss you have to make calls for medical reasons. You are recovering from alcohol, drugs and food, Mia, and you need your sponsor now.

Jennie: It's serious for me too, Mia. It's between life and death now anyway. I have to confess something. I had $10,000 in bills and I got my Bible and put the bills in it and stood on my Bible and prayed for God's help. And yesterday, I got a job for $3,800 a month. I'm so scared, but I have to go back to Phoenix and tell them I will pay my debts. The creditors and the sheriff were after me. But I have to do it—I have to make amends to live....

Mia: I know, what you say...it's the truth...and I won't quit either, Jean. I guess he'll have to fire me first.

Sandy   :If he'd fire you, you could go on unemployment...don't worry about it now—worry about it later if you have to.

Mia: OK.

While confession and amends are considered obligatory by the staff, they are typically met with initial resistance by the patients. However, because this behavior is usually rewarding both through positive staff attention and emotional catharsis, it is increasingly likely to be incorporated into the patient's repertoire. In addition, when a patient deals directly with her unexpressed emotions in the presence of a family member, the interchange may eventually lead to increased understanding and respect. Sam was one of the two male patients on the unit one evening. During family therapy, he chose to display "recovering" behavior by confessing his feelings with his family. The following interchange then occurred:

Sam: ...I am hurt because neither of you [two daughters] really turn to me for anything but business advice.

Alice
[counselor]: Anything else, Sam?

Sam: Yeah, I feel left out of this family.

Margo
[wife]: That's not true, how can you say that?

Sam: I come into the kitchen and you and the girls stop talking....I don't feel like I belong.

Margo: Well, we were talking woman to woman things...and I don't talk about everything with Bob [son not present].

Tim
[another
patient]: I think you are trying to gloss over it...trying to justify your behavior.

Alice: Why don't you [Sam] check it out with your daughters and see if it was womam to woman talk.

Debbie
[daughter]: ...No, it wasn't woman to woman talk. It was asexual really. I just didn't know that you really cared, Dad.

Sam: Well, I do. I love you both.

Debbie and
Kim: [simultaneously] Oh Dad, I love you, too.
[Kim gets up and hugs her father. Sam gets teary eyed and wipes at his eyes. And then he turns to his wife. Sam says, "I love you too, Margo."]

Margo: I love you, Sam.
[Debbie and Kim are crying. Margo looks at them.]

Martha
[another
patient]: What about them?

Margo: Oh, we went shopping today....I showed you that I loved you. [Margo gets up and hugs the girls and then sits down.]

Alice: They need to *hear* you say it!

Margo: I love you, Debbie. [Margo begins crying.] I love you too, Kim. [The girls come over to their mother and hug her.]

Kim: We love you too, Mom.

Often, a patent is required by staff to deal with her negative emotions without the benefit of a significant other present.

Regardless of the circumstances, a patient is obligated to expose her emotions and accept personal responsibility for her own actions. Simultaneously, she is to acknowledge she has blamed others for her problems, through the inappropriate expression of such feelings as sadness, abandonment, and fear. Staff maintain strict control over this process by confronting patients in any available circumstance. In addition to verbal comments, staff is likely to assign tasks and rituals for homework to facilitate the patient's display of appropriate emotion management.

Sandy [counselor]:	Beth, I think you're holding a lot in about your mother. I want you to write a hate letter to your mother telling her what you feel.
Beth:	[teary eyed] I don't hate my mother. I don't think I ever did....
Sandy:	Then why the tears?
Beth:	I don't know.
Sandy:	How did she make you angry?
Beth:	Well, I wasn't often. I remember once when she wouldn't let me go out...
Sandy:	Once?! [incredulously]
Beth:	[laughing nervously] We got along okay. [Beth sits slumped over and looks very sad but defensive.]
Robin:	You look so sad...and lonely. I'd bet you were lonely as a child....
Beth:	[crying openly] My brother was sick as a boy and my mom paid attention to him....I did a lot of the housework...I'd be with my dad. He used to play with me sometimes....One time he dropped my on my head when he was swinging me and I had to get stitches. He died...after my mom did...I didn't know my brother very well, we went to different high schools....I don't see my son since he went to college. I guess I've been lonely all my life. Maybe that's why I'm fat...
Robin:	You haven't mentioned your husband, what about him?
Beth:	He committed suicide two years ago. [She sobs deeply.]
Robin:	What are you still angry about? [I noticed she is clenching her fists in her lap.]
Beth:	[She began rocking back and forth in the chair.] I...I...I am so angry! I am so mad at him! He left me alone with the kids...and the bills...I didn't know what to do and it was so unfair....I felt it was my fault...I should have been there and he wouldn't have...but I didn't know...but maybe I did, I don't know.
Sandy:	What could you have done?
Beth:	I could have gotten us some help...He could have gotten help...and maybe he'd be alive today.
Sandy:	Maybe yes, and maybe no. We will never know. But we do have to go on with our lives and forgive and accept the things we cannot

change....And we can still be sad, and angry too, if that's what we are feeling...and it will pass in time, the horrible hurt will lessen...in time...as you work your program, Beth.

In this and similar instances, staff see the patient as expressing her emotions in an organizationally appropriate style. The staff define her "successful" emotion management as part of the trajectory of recovery. On another occasion, a patient named Suzanne became extremely upset and began to express her intense feelings of rage and resentment toward her abusive (and absent) parent. During a staff meeting, staff discussed her behavior as appropriate and healthy, and thus a part of recovery.

Alice: At first she fell apart quietly when she saw Karen work with the batacas [heavily padded baseball bats used to hit others or objects, theoretically without injury to either party.] She asked to work and she beat the shit out of that chair....She went crazy and threw herself on the floor and screamed and flailed wildly around....It was really intense. I told her she did good work.

Lisa: She needs to work on the anger. Seven hours a day would not be enough.

Jody: OK, for the chart, [she is writing in the patient's chart] what are we saying about Susanne?

Lisa: She's getting in touch with anger and expressing rage.

Sandy: Feeling emotions in very important.

Jody: Shame...getting in touch with feelings from early childhood experiences of neglect, OK? Got that?

Interestingly, whatever expression of emotions used by the patient in the past is likely to be labeled as a "sick" way of handling emotions, but is also now viewed as normal for the process of recovery (with the exception of dysfunctional eating). The vast arena of emotional expression from hostile to withdrawn, from manic to depressed is presented as permissible (and is some cases, necessary) for recovery. Staff thus defines and controls the "emotional rules" for the patients.

For example, the patients are told by staff that "everyone" exhibits negative behaviors and emotions such as those displayed by the patient prior to admission, and that "all those [displays] are really sick." Paradoxically, during institutionalization these same actions are "a healthy sign of getting better." While patients may experience some difficulty accepting this apparent inconsistency, staff are quick to censure any criticism of the SED philosophy. Universality, as

Millman (1980) noted in her research on members of Overeaters Anonymous, at times was stressed to the limit of credibility.

STAFF MEASUREMENT OF WORKING THE PROGRAM

Commitment to working the program is defined as "apparent" effort toward self-transformation: self-stigmatization, appropriate dependency and emotional management. The staff informally measure a patient's success at working her program based on the extent and intensity of her perceived vulnerability and sincerity.

Vulnerability is measured by the staff in terms of the appropriateness of the emotion attached to disclosures, as well as the level of intensity expressed by the patient. Most frequently, crying is used by staff as an index of vulnerability. Overall, crying is seen by staff as a desirable and as a necessary, though not usually sufficient, part of good self-work. For example, on one particular occasion, the clinical director decided to attend a specific family therapy session because the counselors reported that an extremely resistant family was present and caused them difficulty.

Maggie: They are so sick...they don't participate at all, they sit and watch. One of them refuses to come to group consistently and when he does come, he disrupts the group by hitting his sister, and making side comments. I watched the mother with the kids and she's so seductive and slimy...they're all crazy. They never get involved with therapy...or show any emotion, really.

The clincal director attended the session and, by exposing the family's vulnerabilities, the negative impression of this family was eradicated.

Maggie: It was amazing. Mark ["bad son"] came in with a book to read and ignored us. He was really hostile...and Mary worked with him and he broke down and cried.

Mary: Everyone then, in the family started crying. They really opened up on some issues. It was really intense.

All: That's really wonderful. Wow! Great! Sounds like you did some great work in there. They have really changed. Congratulations, Mary. They were tough to crack.

Although crying is used as a key indicator of vulnerability, other expressions of vulnerability are also noted by staff. One such instance concerned a patient named Chris, who was perceived by the staff as "now vulnerable and willing to work to the best of her ability" because of the intensity of her interaction with her husband during a family therapy session.

Dr. C: Chris needs to hear positive stuff. But she takes it in and hears everything and brings it back...

Mary: Chris did come out with feelings. But he [husband] is the one who refuses to move. She beat him with a bataca but he stood there rigid and the whole group told him he was fixed and the one who was not moving. Chris was flushed in her face and really worked and has energy. So I think it all revolves around him. He's the pivot point in the family now. And what he did with it was he took it all in "under advisement, of course" because he's the shrink [Chris's husband is a psychiatrist].

Frequently, patients who do not overtly express their emotions are seen as highly resistant to therapy and defined by staff as very sick. For example, a patient named Megan asked permission to read two letters in group therapy.

Megan: They're both to my parents in New Jersey. One is a hate letter and one is a love letter. [She reads them aloud with little affect. Afterwards she states:] I didn't feel anything...just sort of detached.

Sandy: That's your disease. Until you will let yourself feel, you will be into your disease.

Megan: I know. I'd say before "I want to recover"...but maybe that's not true. I'm getting something out of being sick, I guess.

Sandy: That's right.

Another gauge used by the staff to determine whether a patient is working the program is sincerity. If the staff conclude that a patient is not sincere in her presentation of herself or her work, she will typically face confrontation by staff and peers. Confrontation involves increased staff effort to work with the patient while pressing the individual in all interactive situations to react in a more "honest" style.

[Paula wants to talk about her fear of calling her husband, and is struggling with whether or not she wants to remain married. She concludes that he is a very important person in her life.]

Alice: That's all bullshit. I am so bored.

Paula: [wailing] I'm a failure...yes, you are right, I am full of bullshit...

Alice: Don't do this for my benefit, cause it's sickening. You jump too quickly into "poor me." [You] do it with everyone. It's sickening. I don't want to hear it. I am your therapist, but I won't listen to this crap...tell me the truth, and I'll listen.

Confrontations about sincerity can be very stressful to the staff, but the brunt of it falls on the patient. The staff can and will elicit the support of the other patients in this matter—so that the patient is literally surrounded and then outmaneuvered until she succumbs to the pressure. The discussion which follows involved an aftercare patient named Sarah and her husband Joe.

Ellen: Sarah and Joe, what's going on with you two? You haven't worked in a long time.

Joe: Nothing much...things are okay. I feel tired and drained tonight [sits slouched in chair].

Sarah: Well, I feel uncomfortable.

Ellen: What's wrong?

Sarah: I don't know.

Angie
[patient]:   Are you bored?

Sarah: No.

Terri
[patient]:   Tired?

Sarah: No. I guess I should work. It's just that...I don't know...[bland and whiny voice].

Ellen: What do you want?

Sarah: I don't know...Joe has to work all the time and we talk only about food...[whiny].

Sue
[patient]:   I'd be upset about the work.

Bob
[patient]:   What do you do?

Joe: I work 12 days straight and then get two days off. I like it...and it's been this way since before we were married [slumping deeper in the chair].

Sarah: We've talked about this before. It can't be changed.

Ellen: So what's the matter?

Sarah: I don't know. We never see each other because we go to different OA meetings...and we haven't been together one night really—except sleeping—since I got home from the hospital two weeks ago.

Mac [patient]:	So what are you going to do about it?
	[Sarah justs sits and says nothing.]
Ellen:	What's up Sarah, you look upset.
Sarah:	I don't know...it was too fast.
Terri:	Come on Sarah, you're using the group to do your own work.
Mac:	Yeah. Figure it out for yourself...Either shit or get off the pot, so to speak.
Ellen:	You are such a poor little victim, Sarah, nothing makes you angry.
Sarah:	[voice became louder] I don't see why you have to get angry to make it work.
Ellen:	You don't *have* to get angry—you just need some energy and be honest!
Other patients:	Yeah!
Ellen:	And anger isn't bad. No emotion is unhealthy or bad unless you take it to the extremes.
Sarah:	Well, I don't want to be angry [slouches in seat].
Cathy [patient]:	You remind me of me. You go into looking like a lump, as I used to be, sitting there trying to please everyone...not wanting to make anyone angry, no matter what the cost.
Ellen:	Some are sicker than others...Sarah, you are refusing to move. So if you don't want to work on your own issues—be honest about it. Otherwise, we can't trust you and you'll never get better.
Sarah:	I want to get better. What do you want me to do?
Mac:	Answer your own question. Be honest with yourself. What can you do, Sarah.
Sarah:	I could arrange to be with Joe by skipping a meeting once a week and we can go together to a meeting another night...How's that?
Ellen:	You know best what's right for you. Just be honest with yourself...and then work it out with Joe.

If confrontation fails, the next option available to the staff when they suspect insincerity is to decide that the patient is either unwilling or unable at this time to work the program. The next step will then be termination without a positive recommendation. But if the patient remains in Stage 2, the staff informally measure a patient's success at working the program on her crying and lying. The more a patient cries the more likely she is to be viewed as demonstrating high vulnerability. The less the patient lies the more likely she is to be seen as sincere.

PERSONALITY TRANSFORMATION

Staff pressure for "working the program" is explained to patients as a way of determining the extent of her personality transformation, which, as I indicated, is seen as mandatory for successful recovery from the disease of compulsive overeating. During an education session the clinical director stated,

> We need to accept a lifelong illness that effects our whole lives....We are talking about changing our lives, not just eating....You people tried to quit eating—and you couldn't. So it got you here in an eating disorder unit. But *we* want more. We want to change your life...Food is a symptom of how you are dealing with life. Eating helped you survive and live the myth. What's involved is a total change in your whole life. It's a total transformation, and in OA, we call it a "spiritual awakening." There are stages in accepting the reality of life and how you have been using food in order to cope. And the first stage, as most of you know, involves "hitting bottom" and that's why we make you do a First Step. So you know who you really are and where you really came from as a compulsive overeater who could not manage her own life....

Staff explain "hitting bottom" as a state of total helplessness brought about by awareness that one has been unable to break the vicious cycle of binge-diet-binge behavior. Each compulsive overeater, in order to recover, reached his or her unique low point at a different place, in a different way, but all have to come to what staff designate as a state of "pitiful and incomprehensible demoralization." In that condition, staff believe the patient is most ripe for "surrender" to a program of recovery. For the staff, to surrender is to be accessible to recovery.

Staff assume that "hitting bottom" transpires on the unit, but patients sometimes report "hitting bottom" prior to hospitalization. The problem is one of semantics. There is a private "hitting bottom" before a patient is admitted to the hospital. The patient has to admit she has a problem, otherwise, why volunteer admission to SED? However, once admitted, there is public confession of "hitting bottom" in a reformation ritual staff call the First Step assignment. Generally, staff perceive this formally ritualized "hitting bottom" ceremony as more emotionally intense and comprehensive than any prior private demoralization by the patient.

At the point of "hitting bottom" the patient is encouraged to become aware of her "physical, mental, and spiritual deterioration," because the staff emphasize that this is "a threefold disease." Each patient is reminded of "how you have destroyed yourself by overeating and how your body is suffering physically from your actions." During a patient outing I overheard one of the more "resistant" patients arguing with a staff member. The patient was angry "because you keep saying it's my fault and I think a lot of it has to do with the circumstances." The staff member replied,

> You must admit Suzanne, your behavior [toward food] has not been sane....In fact it's pretty insane to binge and vomit and binge and vomit all day long. Admit that to yourself....You have an emotional problem. You react insanely because you basically have stinking thinking. Therefore, your problems are psychological and of your own making....We address the problem from an emotional and spiritual standpoint by confession and making amends. That's why it's important you work your program. Otherwise, you'll never have a spiritual awakening. And without that, you can't recover.

The means most frequently used to influence the patient to acknowledge that she has hit bottom and then to redefine her past behavior, thoughts and emotions in terms of illness, is through the use of staff storytelling on the unit. Each of the staff shares her autobiography with the patients as a means of encouraging them to selectively recall painful past experiences related to food and eating behavior. For example, in one group sharing session one of the staff stated:

> I equated my self-worth with my food intake and my weight. When I was overeating, I felt "bad" and "worthless." ...I hated myself. I wasn't even able to take care of myself. I was sloppy and disgusting. For me, when I finally admitted this to myself, that was "hitting bottom."

Patients' emergent "hitting bottom" stories are modeled on staffs'. While some patients report "hitting bottom" in terms of an indistinct period of time, most of these women eventually locate some discrete point in their lives when they reached utter "hopelessness." One woman notes, "I remember waking up in the morning after a huge binge the night before. And I wanted to die. It didn't seem worth living anymore." Another patient commented, "I was fed up with losing, then gaining back the weight. I decided it had to stop. I was desperate." One patient summarized her moment of private demoralization as,

> It got to the point when I was sick and tired of being sick and tired and so I was finally willing to go to any length. That's how I knew I'd hit my bottom. And that's when my recovery started.

Although a few of the patients insist they have reached this stage prior to hospital admission, the vast majority are badgered by the staff into "an awareness of their condition." And all patients must go through the same public "stripping and leveling" process (Goffman 1961) in a series of formal procedures such as the First Step assignment. According to staff, once a patient admits powerlessness over food, and surrenders to her Higher Power for assistance, she has had a spiritual awakening.

It is very rare for the staff to acknowledge a spontaneous recovery following a "sudden spiritual awakening." This may be for two reasons. First, to admit to sudden spontaneous recovery would jeopardize their credibility and the necessity for inpatient treatment, and ultimately, their own economic survival. If one can recover spontaneously, why pay $13,000 and spend 4-6 weeks in a hospital? Second, even if there is dramatic overnight process, the staff is very unlikely to dismiss the patient, because of the money they would lose in an early dismissal. In addition to economics, staff has a political reason: they like having a living success-story around on the unit as a role model for others to emulate and because a "transformed" patient is much easier to treat, in turn making them feel successful as therapists.

Medical intervention is specifically stressed as the most effective means to recovery to insurance companies or other third-party payment groups. Recovery is presented as an achievement of therapeutic intervention: something the therapists do effects changes in the patient. What is presented to an outsider is the following position: as a result of hospitalization, an overeater recovers adequately to be discharged to a relatively normal way of eating. She has learned different behavioral modification techniques which will aid her in food selection, eating, weight loss, and weight maintenance.

Although the spiritual aspect is stressed as the primary cause of recovery to patients and their families, on occasion, progress in recovery is attributed to the therapeutic interventions of the staff. Thus the why and how a patient recovers from compulsive overeating may be portrayed as more or less the result of spiritual or medical intervention, depending on the particular audience.

VIGILANCE

After achieving a "spiritual awakening" and begining the process of a complete personality transformation, staff expect a patient to maintain vigilance regarding her "fragile condition."

Throughout hospitalization the staff repeatedly inform patients that

> This is your last chance....You came here because there was nowhere else to go. Out there [beyond the institution's walls] is only insanity or death. You have only three choices: recovery, insanity or death....And you have to be always on guard, because you might slip [relapse].

According to staff, one must maintain vigilance over behavior, thoughts, and feelings in order to analyze them for any pathological symptoms of relapse. However, this vigilance ironically reinforces the patient's awareness of her disease and her precarious position as "recovering," in that all action can potentially be a means of digression from the "true" path of recovery.

The result of this fear of relapse is likely to be excessive vigilance by staff, and extreme patient dependency on and conformity to the OA/treatment program. Patients engage in continous self-monitoring for signs of getting better or worse. Getting worse is labeled "slipping" by the staff.

Alice (counselor) talked with me about Sharon, a patient she was "observing" because staff detected signs of "slipping." Alice mentioned feeling very frustrated with Sharon "because she was doing so good in her work, but now she's making me crazy because she's started to obsess about food again. I'm really worried about her slipping!" Sharon, an anorexic, said she was feeling confused because she didn't know if she had "slipped" by eating three tablespoons of yogurt after authorized snack-time. But she had skipped food earlier, so she was debating whether "It is okay or not okay, I'm not sure."

Alice: You have such control on this, setting it up to be a major problem....Not eating for you is a game just like binging. It's terrible, and yet you play. It's a small game, but it's a cop out, Sharon. You aren't dealing with your feelings. All you want to talk about is the food...to everyone...After your staffing, we [staff] told you how heavy it was that it wasn't working for you and you will either go to a psych ward or go out and starve—you didn't address that. All you want to talk about is the food—just the food...no feelings...

Sharon: Well, maybe I felt panic which is why I ate. I couldn't help it.

Sam and
Karen
[patients]:   But all you talk about is food—all you ever talk about now is food!

Sharon: That's not true. I bounced it off the others....I wanted help. I didn't know if I'd slipped.

Karen: But that's all you did was bounce it off...

Sharon: I tried to take it [their advice] in...I really did. I thought about what everyone said to me.

One obvious function of vigilance is that it makes the patient hyper-aware of her behavior and its "universal" consequences. The typical patient scrutinizes her thoughts, behavior and emotions because of the threat of a relapse or even treatment termination if she should lose control. A patient explained her preoccupation with her behavior during an evening break:

I really want to get well. I can see now how sick I was. And I never want to go back there. It was hell....So I do what they [staff] tell me to do. I take a *continuous* personal inventory—and when I'm wrong, and that's all the time, I promptly admit it and make my amends, like they say to do in the Twelve Steps.

Another patient noted,

You know, they tell us we are never cured, we have a "daily reprieve based on maintaining a fit spiritual condition." I can keep it only by staying on program....And I won't eat any flour or any sugar and I will have three meals a day...Because if I don't watch my food and my actions—then I'll get into trouble, big trouble, with my food again...I can't handle this alone. That's why I have two sponsors. I'm really afraid but I'm depending on my H.P. to help me recover. I can't do it alone...That's dangerous. One of them [staff] calls it suicide.

By reframing her past eating habits as a symptom of the disease, and internalizing continuous vigilance for recovery, the patient develops a self-image full of self-doubt and fear.

For the majority of the patients, constant self-monitoring eventually leads to ambivalent feelings.

> I do a personal inventory every day. But sometimes I can't see how it's my fault. And that scares me....It's my pride. And if my pride gets in the way, I'll go back out and eat again and I'll be dead....I really worry about that— all the time. It's like I'm pulled—a good me and a bad me. And if I'm not careful all the time, I'm doomed...I worry because even though I'm doing it right, sometimes I'm just full of fear that the whole thing will just get totally wiped out if I just do one thing wrong—like one piece of cake....And then I think that's crazy and I start to doubt my program. I mean, what's one piece of cake going to do? And then I know my stinking thinking has control and I better get some help right away. Because a piece of cake is poison!

Staff define ambivalence as a symptom of relapse, especially in the later stage of recovery. Thus in order to be perceived as healthy, the patient has to eventually repress these uncomfortable feelings and display a false image of herself as untouched by any doubts or fears. This dilemma is often resolved toward the end of treatment by the patient reconstructing her biography. This revision usually results in the development of luminary sagas of saintlike behavior and progress, in which recovery appears as a spontaneous miracle or a linear growth pattern with minimal backsliding or plateaus. Luminary sagas are the patients' ultimate response to staff manipulation and control.

To be perceived as "working the program" a patient must embrace self stigmatization, accept the staff definition of what is considered appropriate dependency, display publicly her most intimate feelings, faults and flaws and make some form of amends when appropriate. The goal for working the program successfully is a personality transformation in which the patient "hits bottom," acquires a Higher Power and proceeds to recover in a somewhat stagelike progression. In addition, a patient has to continuously monitor her thoughts, feelings and actions in order to protect her fragile condition of eternally "recovering."

Chapter V

Mechanics of Control Used by Staff

Staff control on SED is reinforced by the liminality that is part of the rite of passage for SED patients. Patients are secluded from the spheres of everyday life, and using Goffman's (1961, p. 140) terms are "leveled" and "stripped" of secular distinctions. They are removed from their social circles and roles. They are "stripped" of material possessions that might represent class distinctions such as expensive jewelry or Rolex watches. Patients are encouraged to wear generic casual attire such as blue jeans or sweat pants, and discouraged from styles and items of clothing that are perceived as professional apparel like business suits and dresses. Maggie, (a counselor) told a new patient the following: "We want you to be comfortable here. So have your husband bring you some play clothes for in here, OK?" In addition, patients are "leveled" in status because all are assigned the common designation of compulsive overeater, and theoretically treated alike. As Turner (1967, p.167) noted regarding the liminal phase, "We find social relationships simplified, while myth and ritual are elaborated." According to the staff, patients must undergo trials and ordeals to teach themselves self-control so that they maintain self-mastery regarding future food temptations.

These processes are analogous to the African installation rituals reported by Turner (1967). The future chief is first separated from the commonalty and then must submit to liminal rites that "rudely abase" him. He is finally installed as the leader in a reaggregation ceremony.

According to Turner (1967 p. 103)

> The ordeals and humiliations, often of a grossly physiological character, to which neophytes are submitted represent partly a destruction of the previous status and partly a tempering of their essence in order to prepare them to cope with their new responsibilities and restrain them in advance from abusing their new privileges.

This chapter investigates the various mechanisms the staff employ to regulate and modify the patient's identity and behavior. There are three types of social control interactions between staff and patients in which the staff seeks to maintain control over the patients and the recovery program. The ultimate goal of these mechanisms of control is to effect the expression of emotions that control eating behavior. These mechanisms are staff observation of patient behavior; rituals of reformation; and normalization ceremonies

STAFF OBSERVATION

During the first few days following admission, staff are aware of patients' sensitivity to, and intense preoccupation with, staff observation of patient behavior. Staff frequently comment that this sensitivity is demonstrated in patients' hesitant verbal responses to staff, as well as frequent informal asides overheard between patients, such as: "I'm really scared. I don't know what they expect." "I feel so nervous...on the spot." "I know they (staff) are watching every move I make." According to staff, it is extremely rare for new patients to openly acknowledge their discomfort to staff. The exceptions are those individuals labeled "retreads" who are experienced "old-timers" in this situation.

Although hesitation and careful monitoring of replies to the staff are characteristic of the newcomers, staff members assert that many of these same patients are likely to assume a more relaxed appearance once they are accustomed to the unit. At the request of her therapist, a patient in group therapy retrospectively analyzed her feelings:

> ...Look. When I came in here last week, I was so damned scared of everyone and everything...especially Sandy [her counselor]. I knew you [staff] were

watching me and it made me very nervous and sort of suspicious of what this was all about....I don't feel that way now. I know you want to help me.

While this statement indicates that staff observation appears over time to be no longer an overtly negative threat to a patient, staff observation remains a covert theme throughout hospitalization. For example, it is very common for a patient to bring even minimal positive behavior changes to the attention of her counselor, "Just in case she didn't notice." Overall, staff view this reporting as useful information and reinforce patients for continuing to do so.

In the eating disorder clinic, behavior dealing with food is the most obvious focus for observation. On occasion, a patient may be caught stealing food from other patients' trays or begging food from her peers. When this is discovered, the patient undergoes intensive surveillance by the staff as well as the other patients. Disobeying eating rules is interpreted as a severe symptom of pathology (not just a temporary relapse), especially if the patient has been hospitalized for a substantial length of time. In addition, if she has previously been labeled a bad patient, she is likely to undergo a punitive ceremony, which is a particular type of reformation ceremony.

Another sign of getting worse is withdrawal from or hostility toward the staff. The following dialogue transpired during a clinical staffing:

Maggie: The next patient [to discuss] is Janie. She's been here one week. She's becoming more hostile and withdrawing from treatment. She's angry and not willing to work...she sat in her group and looked at her feet. I plan to confront her on this.

Mary: She rebels against authority figures.

Dr. C.: Janie puts her anger all over the place and puts off her own confrontation.

Mary: She's no longer compliant, but passive-aggressive. Have you interpreted this for her?

Maggie: Yes.

Mary: Anything else?

Maggie: She's real slippery even when we confront her. She says "OK" and pretends to agree and then she slips out. I think she is getting worse and we'll have to watch her.

Ellen: You have to confront her, too.

Maggie: Right.

At this point, the patient passes from routine observation into the realm of intensive and systematic surveillance. Surveillance means more careful observation of a suspicious nature as well as more thorough documentation in the patient's file. However, a woman could earn surveillance not only through withdrawal or extreme negativity, but for excessive obsequious behavior. Thus, the "good" patient must not deviate too far in either direction. Such was the staff's reaction to Amy Sue.

Maggie: She tries too much! She writes reams of paper and tries to be interested in everyone. She's so nice, squeaky clean and polite. It's like white sugar, tastes good but deadly!

Sandy: She seems immature, not silly though. She's very into people pleasing.

Mary: Kiss ass.

Dr. C.: Do you mean ingratiating? She needs to work on feelings.

Maggie: She's full of shit...dazzles you with fancy footwork even in her first week here! She's had years of therapy and knows all the language.

Dr. C.: She has a hard time expressing feelings.

Maggie: She talks *about* her feelings.

Jody: So the plan is for her to work on getting in touch with feelings and we'll watch her, is that right?

Most patients are unlikely to be placed under intensive surveillance. For the most part, any signs of progress are dutifully noted in their files, while the symptoms of "slippage" are likely to be neutralized in staff sessions. For example, in clinical meeting about a patient who had been on the unit for three weeks, the following conversation took place:

Ellen: Clarice's become very programmy; she intellectualizes a lot more now.

Dr. C.: Part of this is due to her background and former racial issues from her childhood.

Mary: Well, she starts telling us how it should be here—but if we call her on it, she crumbles.

Dr. C.: She told me that she's had to hold things together and put on all the right faces for so long, she doesn't know how to be real...and it scares her because she doesn't know who she is, and she's starting to face this here, now.

Ellen: She has a lot to deal with...but she's working on it, I see.

Jody: So this week is support and encouragement, right?

Thus, the staff neutralize worrisome behaviors by deciding that the patient is working on some painful issue: they interpret these behaviors as a defense mechanism. As long as the staff can justify to themselves that the patient is "working" or seriously attempting to address the troublesome issue, then there is no increase in critical observation. In fact, there is usually an increase in supportive attentiveness toward the patient.

RITUALS OF REFORMATION

The second mechanism of control implemented by the staff concerns various types of activities I will call rituals of reformation, because these rituals are designed by staff to reform patients either emotionally or behaviorally. One category of these rituals involves the entire patient population. This will be referred to as universal rituals. The other classification involves specialized rituals designed for labeled classes of patients.

Universal rituals involve all patients, and frequently include the staff and family members. The first is the repetition of a ritual liturgy in which patients acknowledge to themselves, the staff, and their families that they are compulsive overeaters, powerless when faced with food. This ritual is practiced in every group therapy context at the beginning of the session. A patient also includes a report of a feeling currently being experienced. Acceptable choices are body symptoms, such as "I feel tired," or emotions, as in "I feel angry." Each patient in the group is expected to publicly announce: "My name is (first name only), I am a compulsive overeater, and I feel _____." Staff as well as patients perform this ritual liturgy. Family members involved in therapy sessions, state the following: "My name is (first name only), I am a co-compulsive overeater, and I feel _____." No variation from the above self-assertion is tolerated by the staff.

Staff is usually challenged by hostile new patients and family members as to the necessity of this ritual. The standard response, exemplified by one staff member's statement, is:

> Our reasoning for stating OUT LOUD over and over again that you are a compulsive overeater—or a co-compulsive overeater—is that instead of blaming outside forces for your problems, you will recognize that your pain was created by your own compulsive overeating, or your response to your

> partner—for your co's....You have to hit utter demoralization before you
> can begin to recover...And another thing, you can't just say "I feel good."
> That's not acceptable here. The reason is that "good" is not a feeling. Good
> is a judgement. You don't FEEL good—or maybe you do! [Laughed and
> pretended touching.] Same thing goes for "OK" or "Fine." We want you
> to get in touch with your feelings....Some of you have no idea of what you
> are feeling! And that's because you have been numb for years!

After hearing the staff position, the overwhelming majority of
patients and family members comply with the staff during group
sessions. On rare occasions, I observed a patient temporarily
refusing to adapt to staff wishes by "forgetting" to make her
pronouncement. The patient was immediately reminded by the
staff, as well as by other patients, and the group actually stopped
and waited for her to make her personal declaration before
proceeding with therapy.

In addition to the public proclamation of being a compulsive
overeater or co-compulsive overeater, the new patient or family
member is informed "You are not to speak for the first twenty-
four hours...just listen." This universal restrictive ritual is also
frequently challenged by the newcomer. One incident occurred
during a private orientation session with one patient's family in
which the counselor asked me to assist her. The counselor had
completed her standard introduction to the unit (this event is
scheduled during the educational portion of the family therapy
evening [usually hour two])—when the patient's sister announced:
"I'm really annoyed with all this....And especially at you Sandy
[counselor], for telling me not to speak in the first group tonight."

Patient's
Mother: I think it is highly unprofessional to be told this, because Monday
night Mary [director] and Jody [counselor] asked us to speak. And
then, I was told tonight by Ellen [her counselor] not to share for
two weeks! [angry pause] I really think that orientation should
be before this point. It's totally embarrassing.

Sandy: Well, you know it's a new unit and we've only been in operation
for just a little while....I'm making excuses, I guess. That's just
the policy we have here, now.

Later, in the clinical records room, Sandy told me that the
patient's sister "was just embarrassed and I apologized...so it's
OK....I am surprised though by her attitude because she [patient's

sister] shared so much in group earlier...it's great she's so willing to work."

Within the first few days of hospitalization, staff inform the patients of mandatory homework assignments, another form of universal reformation ritual. Three tasks are assigned by the staff as nightly obligations. The first is to read the designated pages from the "Big Book" of Alcoholics Anonymous and to write "what you got out of it." Staff encourage brevity because the counselor who reviews each patient's journal had told staff she "was sick and tired of them all saying the same thing over and over." Next, patients read and write on the assigned pages in the "Little Book" of thoughts entitled *For Today* (1982). And, third, patients are to write their feelings on how they felt throughout the day. All of this material is written on only one front of one journal notebook page, finished every evening, and turned in to the the appropriate staff in the morning.

However, the homework that requires the most time and dedication to complete are the projects labeled the First Step and the Fourth Step. These Steps are the guidelines set down for recovering alcoholics in Alcoholics Anonymous and are adapted to fit compulsive overeaters. This ritualized task requires a patient to compose an intensive and personal series of self-assessments as to the cause and consequences of her compulsive overeating.

The First and Fourth Step Assignments

The First Step is "We admitted we were powerless over food—that our lives had become unmanageable." In addition, powerlessness is extended to other people. Staff suggest that the patient "learn to let go and stop managing the affairs of others." In this assignment, she is also asked to "admit that she is not humanly capable of managing her own life—that she needs help."

Using the First Step as a blueprint for self-exploration, each patient writes an inventory composed of an autobiography about herself and her "disease." It is a historical account of when the problem of overeating first began. The First Step assignment is usually written in a patient's journal, which is shared in group therapy or read periodically by the staff in order to monitor homework assignments and signs of progress. Specific material from these assignments is examined in the following chapter,

"Storytelling," which analyzes the patients' responses to the mechanisms of staff control.

Staff somberly inform each patient that their journal is an "autobiography about yourself and your disease—and it starts with when the problem began for you. The First Step is admitting you have a problem, writing about it...the First Step is an admission." Instead of "blaming outside forces" for a patient's problems, staff insist that "she be made to recognize that her suffering and shame had been created by her own compulsive overeating."

The Fourth Step assignment is actually a continuation of the First Step. The Fourth Step requires the patients to make "a searching and fearless moral inventory" of themselves. They are to address their deep or hidden "character defects" that have caused their overeating behavior. One counselor explained the Step assignments to me as follows:

> It's a conversation with you and your feelings—like anger or resentment...or with a problem. You write it like a dialogue, in your journal. Treat it as another person and talk to it...and you'll be surprised what comes out of it.

In another conversation with staff members, I again raised the subject of the Step assignments. Alice was the first to respond.

Alice: We give them a First Step to write so they can face their powerlessness over food and how their life is totally unmanageable....

Robin: What if they lie?

Maggie: I never thought of that. They never lie....I don't think on the First Step that they lie...they lie on lots of other things though....

Ellen: They do dialogues with themselves to confront themselves.

Maggie: I used to write reams—all self—pity—until the end and then talk program but it's really bullshit. The dialogues are really honest...where I have to be RESPONSIBLE for what I say—my part of it...my behavior...

Ellen: This is a great program, but I'm predjudiced...It's really a great program and it really works but it's not a spa or health club. We don't concentrate on food or weight but on feelings because we distort and eat down our feelings...we don't share feelings....There is a saying around here, "Our thinking got us here." We distort our thinking....

Patients are not the only ones assigned to this particular task. All family members who attend the family therapy sessions are also required to write Step assignments. Staff inform family members that they are to read aloud their work during their first group therapy session. A counselor told me:

> We want the co's [co-compulsive overeaters] to talk in the groups and share their stories and First Step so they can get feedback from others about what they are saying...

Usually, when a spouse shares his First Step assignment, attention is directed to the specific ways and means he'd attempted to control his wife's eating behavior. One such speech, by a spouse named Walter, is presented below in an abbreviated version:

> I tried to be in control....I didn't know she was a compulsive overeater when we got married. That was ten years ago and it's been a bummer for me and the kids....She asks me to help her with food—to hide it, lock it up, chart her weight loss when she's dieting, and I do it...I used to think I did it for her. But now I can see I was doing it for me. I guess I am nuts, too....It makes me crazy just watching her eat! One time I even took her to a motel to live so she wouldn't be tempted...I'd buy special food for her and it'd make me crazy cause she wouldn't eat it. And do you know why? Because she'd gone out and eaten earlier—sneaking out of the house and lying to me to me or the kids...it was nuts at our house...And then, she'd cry and I'd feel sorry for her and I'd be hooked and I'd do it again...And our sex life was just as crazy. I never knew what was happening there either. She'd just be numb a lot....I knew she was unhappy and I couldn't fix her...and damn it, I'd just keep trying, all the harder...

Upon completion of this exercise, staff expect those present to immediately respond to the spouse's First Step by revealing how his statement reflects their own past behavior and personal experiences. Frequently, the first to speak has been in the group for the longest period of time. For example, during one therapy session, the following dialogue transpired:

> Pat: I can really relate to what you said. I did that to my wife, too.
> Paul: It's like you were telling my story, Walter.
> Connie: I feel so sorry for you...Because you look so lost and sad—just like I did when I got here...

If no one responds, the therapist makes a comment to elicit interaction. Patients and family members usually share first and then the therapist summarizes, for the spouse, whether or not she feels the spouse had made a sincere and serious effort at his First Step. The staff member then makes her own personal affirmation of the program. In Walter's case, the counselor stated:

> Sandy: You worked very hard in here tonight, Walter. I only say you working so hard one other time...I think you did a good First Step in acknowledging your powerlessness over Nora [his wife]....So much of my life was a major catastrophe. I had to learn that no one is perfect out there or in here. But for me, my marriage is so much better than in the past—because of this program...My husband and I had a fight last night and he hit me [shows bruises to the group]. But it's better than in the past and what I've done to him...
>
> Walter: [interrupting Sandy with a shocked voice] You've been in OA for so long! I thought your marriage was perfect.
>
> Sandy: Well, [laughing] you can see it's not. But it's so much better than in the past...we'd tear each other apart...practically kill each other...I'm really grateful for this recovery program...

While the majority of First Steps recited by spouses are litanies of food or weight control issues, on occasion the co-compulsive overeater declares himself unaffected in these areas. In this instance, the spouse is encouraged to address how his wife has made his life unmanageable. One example was Bob, who shared:

> I don't have problems with her food or weight. I don't care. My main problem is how she makes my life unmanageable...She screams and yells at me and I act like a zombie. I come in and sit in front of the TV and ignore her. I haven't felt anything for a long time. It's like I've shut down....She can be wonderful, we like to travel and she works for the airlines...but other times it's awful. The last five years it's gotten worse and worse and I can't stand it...We've been married 32 years and have three grown children...and she starts these tirades and I shut down...

The therapist responded by suggesting that he was running away from his feelings and that unless he faced the situation there would be no permanent improvement.

> Bob: Yes, that's how it is. It's a lot like how I feel...I have been hurt but it was a long time ago. I really don't feel anything now...

His therapist asked him to "write about the pain you are aware of...your bewilderment at watching her go from a size 5 to 175 pounds..." Bob responded:

> Yeah, I really don't understand how she can do a diet one month and then later gain it back the next.

Bob acknowledged his wife's size and eating behavior was confusing to him but then insisted it "doesn't bother me...it's her attitude that's getting to me."

While all of the patients comply with the Step rituals, there is a much lower response rate among family members. Staff continually comment on the lack of family follow-through during the education sessions. One evening, a staff member told family members during education that:

> The patients' recovery depends on family participation and cooperation—not only by coming to the groups—but by doing your assignments as well...if you want them to recover—you have to see your part in this too. And you can't do that without doing a First and Fourth Step....

When I inquired what becomes of these inventories collected from the patients and family members, I was informed by the unit secretary and two paraprofessional counselors that:

> Mary keeps the co's First Step, because she's planning to write a book. We put the dialogues, pictures [of the patients on their first day of admission to the unit], First Steps and anything like that of the patients in a folder—not in the chart. And they get that when they leave here. It's theirs.

Gentle Eating

Another of the universal reformation rituals is "Gentle Eating." Gentle eating is taught by a staff member or a volunteer helper from OA during lunchtime four days a week. Although Gentle Eating is formally espoused when staff are with patients, only the clinical director occasionally appeared to practice this ritual during meals when patients were not present. This highly ritualized experience makes the patient intensely aware of the eating process. The staff say that the purpose of the restrictions is to create a deliberateness to the meal in order to slow the patient's eating. As one clinician noted:

> It becomes a contemplative experience....Food actually takes on a new meaning because you're forced to study each bite from the moment you pick up the food until you swallow.

Rules for gently eating are: No talking, no water, no salt, no fork permitted in the hand while chewing food, and no swallowing until the food is LIQUID. Water is not served with the meal because "it just helps to pour the food down your throat...diluting the natural saliva of the month." Patients are told to make a conscious effort to leave something on their plates. This is because they are "in the habit of inhaling their food." Soft music is played for the patients as they eat the bland hospital fare on thick, white glass plates with little plastic forks. They are told the plastic forks slow the "shovel-arm response" that often accompanies the use of regular silverware. The fare for this occasion is a "salad" consisting only of a piece of chopped iceberg lettuce, approximately two-thirds cup of cooked carrots, two slices of white turkey meat (four ounces), and a 12 ounce can of generic diet soft drink. There is no butter or other condiment on the tables. One counselor informed me later "the patients really abuse this stuff [condiments]—so we don't have it here."

On the first staff-patient outing that I attended, the food for lunch consisted of 4 ounces of boiled chicken, a half cup of cooked cauliflower, two baby tomatoes, several sticks of raw carrot and celery, a diet soda, and *mustard*. Mustard became the center of my table's entire meal conversation. Patients intently discussed the meaning of the lack of condiments provided for them. One patient told the others at the table:

> We used to have it [mustard] all the time, but not anymore...because people ate it by the spoonfuls....Then it was soy sauce. When we got to have that, everything was swimming in soy sauce. So they took that away, too. Now we have hot sauce...but we've had that for a while...probably because no one can stand too much of it!

From this conversation, and numerous similar discussions, it is apparent that Gentle Eating has the immediate effect of concentrating the patient's attention totally on her food and slowing down the eating process. However, it is apparently not successful in eliminating the food obsession, perhaps because it focuses attention on food.

Many of the patients privately remarked "It's kind of boring after a while...but I'd have to admit I don't gulp my food as fast as before." Others reported they were "more aware" of food's relationship to their bodies as well as their feelings. Several stated some variation of the "food is only fuel for the body" theme and further noted it was in the past that they attributed some type of comfort and/or consolation with food. The majority believed the gentle eating exercise has helped them "get food under control." One patient summarized this process when she stated:

> Like everyone else, I really hated gentle eating at first...it drove me crazy...everyone is so quiet and those damn little plastic forks...but I can see some good in it now. I used to eat automatically, in front of the TV or reading the paper....I think when I get out of here that's something I won't do anymore....And I used to gulp down Twinkies and ice cream when I was upset about something. I think that automatic reaction won't be so strong when I'm out of here....I'm more in touch with my feelings now, and I'll catch it before it [overeating] happens.

Staffing

A final universal ritual of reformation the staff present to patients is the formal progress staff meeting. "Staffing" is a carefully orchestrated procedure in which the patient receives direct verbal feedback from the entire staff on her progress in treatment. This event is usually held between the fourteenth and twenty-fifth day of treatment.

The therapists rehearse their speeches prior to addressing the patient. The chairs are arranged in a semicircle with the patient's chair at one end facing the group. Everyone maintains silence unless directly addressing the patient. The patient is not permitted to respond to the feedback except to affirm that she has understood what she has been told by staff.

The following staffing involved a patient named Candy on her eighteenth day on SED. As the newest addition to staff, it was my duty to escort Candy to her staffing. As I got to her room, she was in her robe and shower cap, putting on her makeup. When I informed her that she was to be staffed, she immediately began to dress and expressed annoyance that she didn't have "enough time to comb my hair!" She then told me she was "very nervous...scared to go in there...." She followed me to the room. I opened the door and walked in, and Candy followed. Sandy told me to "lock the door before you sit down." For several seconds there was complete silence. Then Sandy spoke.

Sandy: Candy, you've been making great progress...you've done good work in group and we'd all like to see that continue....You've shared some very private things about your family...had major insights...we're going to give you a pass for tomorrow to be with your husband. You can go to a motel, go shopping, go to the beach—whatever...leave at ten and be back after dinner together, by six p.m. for group.

[Candy looked very happy and excited. She smiled and sat toward the edge of her seat.]

Ellen: You really had a major breakthrough yesterday with feelings— but you aren't going to be discharged until next week, even though you expected it Thursday, because we want you to integrate and relax with your new information and how you can deal with anger.

Doctor: I agree.

Mary: We are all happy with your progress.

Sandy: You can go now. Robin, open the door for her, OK?

I got up and unlocked the door. Candy left the room with a broad smile on her face.

The vast majority of "staffings" have a positive tone and end with the ultimate reward of a pass being granted for "good work." Of course, passes are awarded only to "good girls," improving "blobs" and reformed "bitches." Some patients are selected to be staffed but the pass is always denied because the patient is "not ready for the responsibility." These patients are perceived by staff as not showing much progress, but having some potential for recovery. For example, Rosemary, identified as a controlling bitch, had been on the unit for sixteen days and was scheduled for "staffing." During the regular staff meeting, the therapists discussed her case:

Jody: ...she's had a horrendous childhood.

Maggie: And now she brings in how important it is for her to be a social worker and take care of others...

Sandy: She has four thousand issues. She makes lots of phone calls...so I told her I didn't like her being such a special case, so she's to make a list of all the calls she needs to make...

Maggie: I think she needs to write a letter.

Mary: Tell her it has to be stopped by Friday and, if not, then she has to go home and work it out—then she can come back...they [her creditors] can wait...it's not punitive...she tried to get in here one year ago...I'll nail her tomorrow in staffing—she works but she gets distracted and goes back to the old way....We want her to write letters and mail them and that's it...she can turn it over to her H.P. We're going to tell her "Don't waste the bedspace"—she either works here or not...All she needs to do is say [to her creditors] "I'm a hospital patient"—but she's acting like an administrator. She's in denial and that's her defense....

Sandy: She's not progressing. She should have no pass because there is no closeness and trust. Tell her, "You need to think and talk about that you can't [be close or trust]."

Mary: She should be told that she has a lot to overcome and will be here a long time...we'll tell her very lovingly in staffing tomorrow.

Jody: ...she needs to get a sponsor, too.

Mary: No pass, right? [Everyone nodded.]

Mary: She needs to shape up and then [we'll] give her strokes for getting better.

In cases such as Rosemary's it is common practice to "come down harder" for the first staffing and then within a week to ten days to have a subsequent and more positive staffing. At this second ritual, she is usually told that there has "been remarkable progress" and a pass is issued at this time.

A very small group of patients, made up almost exclusively of slimeballs and crazymakers, are periodically told by staff that they would not be scheduled for a staffing. The most frequent reason cited is that the patient has not shown "any sign of progress." One particular patient, named Sheila, had been on SED for thirty-four days and had not been officially given her staffing.

Mary: She doesn't want to recover, does she?

Sandy: She's exercising in her room...and confronted by two patients and she lied about it...she's taken extra yogurt...

Doctor: She doesn't want to be aware of her feelings...

Mary: She should not be staffed—no progress...

Sandy: Maybe she should be sent to a mental institution.

Doctor: That might help us, but not her...

Mary: Custodial care—she will be here because she made no progress.

Doctor: I'm still concerned about her suicidal part.

Sandy: We keep telling her she is [making] progress, but she's not...

Mary: So why the charades? She shouldn't be staffed...her husband...he's got "so good" all over him.

Ellen: He's a nice slimeball...a pain in the ass—he's a typical jerk.

> Jody: He's always the adult parent and she's treated like the young child....

Nine days later, Sheila had been in the hospital for forty-three days with no reported progress. The staff was experiencing "severe burnout" with her case and several labeled her as "hopeless."

> Ellen: She says she's unwilling. That's it. "I am unwilling [to work]."
> Mary: Discharge her with a poor prognosis and do it.
> Doctor: Do you mean, tell it and not do it?
> Mary: Do it.
> Ellen: She's loving her role here.
> Jody: She thinks she's winning here and we should tell her that.
> Sandy: She shouldn't be staffed...she's winning the battle but losing the war.
> Mary: Passive aggressive—loser position...have group members try to break through the resistance and help her. But she is to get nothing from the staff...[we'll] give her sadness.

Universal rituals of reformation are designed for the entire patient population of the unit. Each patient is encouraged, and in some cases compelled, to participate in these universal rites and tasks in order to facilitate the expression of those emotions said to control eating behavior. The following section deals with the special reformation issues that were tailored to fit an individual patient's particular circumstances and needs.

Specialized Reformation Rituals

Although theoretically designed for each individual, specialized reformation rituals are likely to be related directly to the informal patient labels identified by the SED staff. Thus, there are specific ritual assignments for the "good girls," "bitches," "blobs," and the "slimeball/crazymakers."

The are nine assignments frequently given to good patients with high potential. Examples of these ritualized tasks range from a patient not being permitted to hug another [male] patient because she is "such a people pleaser," to an exercise in which the patient is to "be dirty for twenty-four hours." According to a staff member, the "be dirty" assignment was given because an individual patient was perceived as being:

Very perfectionistic...she needs to let go of showering and always fixing her hair...she needs to be allowed to have inappropriate behavior, so she can get in touch with her feelings.

The most frequently assigned ritual for "good girls" is one titled "Be A Child." This exercise is a means for the staff to challenge the patient's rigidity in her people pleasing and/or care taker role. For example, the dialogue below concerned a "good girl" named Pam:

Jody:	In group today, Pam got in touch with never acting like a child. She got teary when Glenda talked. She's always been such a good producer. I think she needs an experience acting like a child.
Sandy:	She's got a physical wad of pain on her chest....Ellen got up and pressed on it and it came out....
Jody:	So what did we hear?
Sandy:	We heard pain and sadness. We asked her to go to each one of us and ask for something she wanted. I thought she was going to throw up....
Jody:	She said she felt sick.
Ellen:	She did a dialogue with the lump that is sadness that she swallows down.
Sandy:	She wanted to play jacks. Maybe it's time for her to develop her childlike side.
Mary:	Giver her an assignment to act childlike. But the problem is lack of spontaneity, too.

Five days later, Pam was dressed for her "Be A Child" role. She wore bright blue shorts and a neon pink tee shirt. Her white knee socks were pushed down to her ankles. She had freckles painted on her cheeks and a bright purple bandana tied in her hair. Pam entered the first group session laughing. Initially, she sat in the folding chair alternately sitting cross-legged, or putting one foot under her thigh and swinging her other leg. She smiled at anyone who made eye contact with her and giggled. However, as the group session became more intense, she became more serious and sat quietly in her seat and listened to others sharing. She made no comments during the session.

Overall, the entire staff was pleased at the appearance and behavior of the "childlike" Pam. They felt she had enjoyed her role playing and "learned how to relax more and be herself." During the length of her three-day assignment, there were no incidents of Pam acting inappropriately either on the ward or in public. One member of the staff noted during a staff meeting,

> She got in touch with the childlike part of herself—without having to act childish. She did it very well, don't you think?...Don't forget to bring it up in her staffing, she'll be leaving here soon....

Patients are strongly encouraged to be creative and active with this task. In many instances, this results in patients acting in ways that outsiders experience as inappropriate, puzzling and immature. Sandy reported on one such scenario which occurred when a counselor took a vanload of patients to an open meeting of Overeaters Anonymous outside the unit.

> Sandy: Sally was throwing paper airplanes and Ron kept clapping when everyone stopped...and then he got up on a folding chair and pretended to be an airplane! It was so funny watching everyone [outsiders] watch him and not say a thing...just sat there with their mouths open...we [staff members and patients] about died trying to keep from laughing at them....He did a great job on his assignment...
>
> Alice: I'd have loved to have been there!
>
> Maggie: My God, what did Edith say? [Edith was a silver-haired, matronly dressed Jewish lady who was the secretary for this particular OA meeting.]
>
> Sandy: She was white. Absolutely white. [Laughter by several staff members.]

In some instances patients are given more than one ritualized task simultaneously. However, whenever the patient is perceived as a "good girl," the assignment of "Being A Child" is seen as priority; self-change is attributed to this ritual. This was demonstrated in the case of a patient named Liz:

> Maggie: I took her off helping everyone because that's what she does so she doesn't have to look at herself....Now she says she's fixed [cured]...she takes in information intellectually and tries to be well...just like Emily. They're both doing the same thing.
>
> Ellen: She's not initiating her own issues.
>
> Mary: Her voice drives me crazy...so whiny and she sits like a PTA mother, so proper—I'd like to see her sit with her legs open and pick her nose! She's so in control.
>
> Maggie: "Excessive appropriateness and inability to tolerate any ambiguity" should be put in her file.
>
> Jody: "Excessive appropriateness" means inappropriate.
>
> Maggie: Right. So I'll tell her to act like a child and we'll see what happens.

Two weeks later, during a staff meeting:

> Maggie: We weren't getting anywhere with her and then Liz went through a major breakthrough. I had her wear her clothes inside out. It almost flipped her out and her husband too....She got real angry and almost left after staffing. She "heard" she wasn't doing well, so she got upset. She said, "Why don't you ask me? Why all these questions about Dick [husband]?"
>
> Sandy: She's afraid he's going to leave her so I suggested [she write] a hate letter to her husband and then she got so upset, I said to make it to us then.
>
> Maggie: The next day, she came into group with a two page hate letter to Dick that was electric! I mean it was hot! I told her she was afraid to recover not because Dick might leave her but that she might leave Dick.

Although the hate letter assignment was described as "electric," the staff unanimously attributed this patient's "breakthrough" to her "child" assignment. Wearing her clothing inside and out was perceived as a direct challenge to her normally controlled and overly appropriate adult behavior. And, as one staff member noted concerning this patient, "She would never have worked so hard on that letter without it [the Act Like A Child Exercise]. That's what did it, Robin. You better believe it!"

The second type of assignment is specially designed for the hostile and resistant "bitches." Because the vast majority of "bitches" are highly verbal with their criticism, the most frequently assigned ritual is "Silence." Patients are told "we [staff] are putting you on twenty-four hour silence...so you can be open to learning something...."

Most "bitches" are openly hostile to this assignment. Therefore, staff make a direct challenge to the patient's professed self-control. One example was a patient named Margaret:

> Margaret: I don't know what you're talking about! I listen. You just have nothing to say that's really important....I don't need to be on silence!
>
> Ellen: Hold on. Wait a minute. You've just cut me off again. You won't listen as long as you have to have a fast comeback.
>
> Margaret: That's not true!
>
> Ellen: Wait! Now, I know this assignment is tough. And, really, it's going to be extra tough on you....In fact, I don't know if you could do it for twenty-four hours....

Margaret: Of course I could, who do you think you are?

Ellen: I'm the therapist. And you are here because you are very sick. And you want to get better, right?

Margaret: Of course.

Ellen: Well, I'm telling you you have to do that. But it's going to be rough—I don't know if you can handle it.

Margaret: I can. Of course, I can.

Ellen: OK. We'll see. You start now.

In some cases, in addition to silence, a patient wears a sign around her neck warning others about the patient's condition. Bill was a locally famous surgeon whose sign stated "I AM THE PATIENT." When I asked about his sign, one staff member said,

> When he got here he played the therapist...that meant he didn't have to expose anything. But he was full of grandiosity, so we told him to put away his $14,000 Rolex and the superior act...he got angry and belligerent. A real asshole. And then he shared about his dysfunctional family. Did you know his father constructed a shock machine to stop Bill's bedwetting— no wonder he still has insomnia.

After the exercise, Bill told me he still wanted to continue wearing his patient sign around his neck "because it reminds me that I'm the patient and to shut-the-hell-up and listen." He noted, "People have always listened to me...I had all the answers...that was the worst thing to do to me—shut me up...but the best thing for me."

One of the more challenging variations to the "Silence" assignment is the ritual of "Assume the Position." Those rebellious patients who are showing some signs of potential vulnerability are likely to get this task.

One example was an extremely angry patient named Cissy, who was sobbing as she shared information concerning her past and her alcoholic father in a group session. The therapist told Cissy that she was "open to receiving" and that Cissy should "assume the position." This meant that Cissy was to stand erect before her peers and cross her arms across her chest. At that point, the therapist stated:

> Once you've assumed the position, I want you to go up to those you want a hug from—and don't try to be such a tough little bitch—you don't have to ask everyone here. But no talking.

Cissy went first to the therapist, and then to the three men in the twelve member group for a hug. She then went back to her seat. She had a radiant smile and was much calmer in her breathing and relaxed in her posture for the rest of the session.

The most challenging assignment for a bitch is a task called "Be An Urn." Usually performed within the intimate setting of group therapy, there are instances when a patient is expected to "Be An Urn" publicly.

While having a break between sessions in the staff room, Alice informed me that Rosemary was assigned to be an urn. When I inquired what that meant, Alice said:

> You have to go up to people and say to them "I am an urn. My urn is empty. I need a hug-or-Can I have a hug?" And then it's up to them to hug you. You aren't allowed to talk or to hug back. You have to just stand there and take it.

I then asked the purpose of the exercise. Alice responded:

> It's incredible. This [exercise] breaks them down so fast. I mean, they are so tough, like steel. And they just go to pieces and cry like babies....They need to be ready, though, or it won't work. If they just do it with the attitude of "this sucks"—that'll never work.

As we walked out of the staff room, Rosemary came up to me and gave her speech. She stood with her hands at her sides and I hugged her. She said "Thanks. You give good hugs." Then she walked away. Alice, who was standing behind me, commented:

> Rosemary's had to deal with rescuing her mom and all these people in her life [she's a social worker]...She's always giving—that's why she's resentful and so angry all the time—she needs to get some [love]...

The next specialized group of assignments are for the "blobs." This group is composed of good patients having a low potential for recovery. Blobs are assigned tasks that are action oriented in order that they may demonstrate some initiative in their treatment. Staff want the "blobs" to more conspicuously participate rather than neutrally assume the recovering identity of compulsive overeater. There are six rituals commonly given to these patients. The least challenging ritual in terms of patient creativity is the

"Fuck You" assignment. The patient responds to any patient or staff member with the words "Fuck You"—regardless or whether the other is asking a question or making a comment within the patient's hearing. No other response is allowed. The therapeutic purpose of this exercise is to "free up" the patient "so she can express anything she wants." Staff believe the blobs need to practice aggressive behavior in order to reach a middle ground of "wholesome" assertiveness.

Ellen:	I sense that June is angry, but she's so nice and bland all the time....
Maggie:	How about a Fuck You assignment?
Ellen:	How about a Bratty assignment?
Maggie:	That's Fuck You.
Sandy:	June has real problems being sexual with her husband—she's coy and embarrassed. She spent the day with her husband last week because she was assigned to have a romantic day. It was okay. But this week she would like a pass to be with her little boy.
Nikki:	Maybe it's time for her to leave...
Sandy:	Maybe assign her this week on loosening up with a Fuck You assignment then release her Friday. She is a sweetie. I hate to see her go.
Jody:	OK, everyone?
All:	OK.

One of the most creatively challenging exercises that staff gave blobs is to act out the role of a vamp. This ritual is assigned when the staff perceives sexual seductiveness as one the patient's problems.

Maggie:	Megan came in so blah...she said to me "When I'm not here, I want you to tell me." I said forget it. I won't be responsible for it. Then she said it was all my fault.
Ellen:	You?
Maggie:	Yes. She said I did it...she has no energy at all....I told her I don't want anything to do with her. She's disgusting!
Jody:	I don't want to make a value judgement.
Maggie:	I will. She's disgusting. She asked for a pass. I don't think she needs it.
Jody:	I don't agree. I think she's very frightened and has no tools at all.
Nikki:	I think she's really condescending.
Ellen:	Maybe she needs to risk more, but we need to really challenge her in order to motivate her to move! She's been here twenty days.

> She has such a blank appearance....It obviously is low self-esteem
> regarding her personal appearance. And there's the incest issue—
> her father used to lay down with her and stroke her leg and look
> at her breasts. She's very scared of being mature and facing sex
> issues...Remember we had Laurie dress and do a strip...act out
> the vamp because the sexual/sensual person is subdued. Megan
> needs to do this kind of behavior.

Three days later:

> Ellen: Finally the behavior is catching up with dressing up because she
> acted more the vamp today—not just in what she had on...but
> still not as risky as she could be....She should have no pass because
> there's just no closeness and trust. Tell her "You need to think
> and talk about that you can't be close or trust."

Staff chooses the "Superior Bitch" exercise as the most effective means of developing assertion in the blob. This exercise is enacted much more frequently than any other assignment given to blobs. It is also the most popularly assigned task on the unit, surpassing the frequently assigned "Be a Child" assignment. The Superior Bitch was in fact the favorite assignment of one of the paraprofessional counselors, and the clinical director had to remind her on several occasions not to give out this assignment so freely. Director to the therapist:

> I know you'd like her to have the Superior Bitch, but Cathy has the Bitch
> assignment and I don't want everyone on the floor at one time [doing the
> assignment]...

The Superior Bitch is for those individuals who are perceived as being dependent, weak, and people pleasers of the bland variety. These patients are to make comments and gestures to other staff and patients throughout the day that would be considered highly inappropriate in another context. The patients assigned the Superior Bitch receive much encouragement from staff and patients even though the assignment frequently is very irritating to others.

The Superior Bitch assignment is subdivided into categories. In the first category, a patient is to confine her bitching behavior to the group therapy setting. She is to go around the room to each of her peers and any staff who are present and make a snide or sarcastic comment to each individual. She is not to apologize for hurting anyone's feelings. An example was a patient named Terry. During staffing the following conversation occurred:

> Sandy: She tries to get As here. She says she can't breathe. I gave her an assignment to be a bitch and to be herself...she's scared and real honest....I asked her to be naked to the other members about her feelings.
>
> Mary: I think we need to stop the performing.
>
> Sandy: I'm working on being more accepting of self with her.
>
> Mary: Make her be a fool and inappropriate in every group. I want dead silence—no one give her response or feedback because then she responds to them saying she was a good idiot.

Later in the converstion:

> Mary: Have you had her go around and tell a bitch to everyone? She's really hard to help because she'll do a bitch well to help her get a good grade. So inappropriate...and no feedback or response from us. Let's see how she does this.

The second classification involves a more all encompassing and diffuse role in which the patient must act in ALL situations "as a real bitch!" The clinical director told one patient who was assigned this role that she (the patient) was expected to:

> Spit it out...confront everyone...say what's on your mind and not hold anything back. And if someone gets hurt because you let someone have it—too bad. Don't apologize!

Donna was another example of this second category.

> Maggie: Donna has been bullshitting all week and then yesterday she seemed to go through a big catharsis in group...
>
> Sandy: She worked in group very well.
>
> Jody: OK, so she's dealing with things.
>
> Maggie: No. I think she's just intellectualizing. She's trying to understand, but it's not working. So, I gave her a bitch assignment last night to dialogue with her superior bitch and to act that way for twenty-four hours. She's started this morning, and doing a great job. Obviously willing...in fact, she was on bitch assignment when we went to an OA meeting outside the hospital this afternoon. Donna went up to the secretary at the Thursday meeting and said,

"I want Maggie to lead this meeting." The lady freaked out because this weird woman didn't want her to speak but rather wanted me to lead the meeting...To back Donna up, I played it straight, and didn't explain anything to the lady. And then I told the OA lady that she should look at why she's so upset about this stranger's comments and then we both sat down...Donna was just so up front and cool. I really admired her work.

On some occasions a patient is perceived as not having done a good job in her role playing. In such a case the therapists are likey to become discouraged and hostile toward the patient in later interactions.

Sandy: Alicia's been here four and a half weeks already, so I assigned her to be a bitch...seems like she's only been here for two weeks— she's not working. I had her go around the group and be bitchy to everyone and then, she kept saying: "[bitch comment], OK? She wasn't doing it right at all. It's frustrating. Then she told Crystal she had nothing really to say to her and then Crystal said sarcastically "You could say OK," she just took it. Such a blob...She's a real contrast to Crystal because at least you've got something to work with. Oh, Crystal's tough all right, and I wonder what she'll do later...but I'd rather not be bothered by Alicia. She's such a wimp. It's sickening.

When a blob is generally unsuccessful in the Superior Bitch role her behavior is seen as frustrating and disappointing to the therapists. However, if this behavior occurs under conditions that are not sanctioned by the therapists, it is considered "acting out" and interpreted as regression. Theoretically, if unsanctioned, this would be cause for serious repercussions, such as expulsion from the unit. However, in no instance did "a blob ever get that bad." Rather, acting out by a blob causes staff to reevaluate their prescription. For example,

Alice: I came on Sunday and I felt the exercises were awful. Lisa was on assignment to be bitchy, it was awful...acting out in the van— no way! Patients were really pissed...they didn't have the outlet of the group to let it loose...I was driving the van—she was really aggravating me. My issue with her was smiling—I think it was slimy. The smile was to devalue her own angry feelings...

Maggie: I apologize. It's inappropriate to give this assignment on the weekend.

Sandy: I think the feelings of everyone need to be dealt with so it's better if there is a group for them....

Mary: We're giving them two messages—(1) it's saying let it out, but (2) it's dangerous without us.

Alice: No. I think they just need the outlet of the group...when she [Lisa] started grabbing knobs—I couldn't handle it...I was driving...she really liked that Superior Bitch role.

Beth: It's hard for her to get out of it.

Alice: The patients need to be given permission to tell her off...

Beth: So they don't sit on it because they are afraid to confront if someone is on an assignment.

Alice: ...they were all huddled in the group room hiding from Lisa...

Overall, the primary task for good girls and blobs is to "DO" something, while the focus for the bitches is "DO NOT" do something. These rituals challenge and arouse the performer and her audience. However, they pale in comparison to the anxiety evoked by the punitive reformation rituals assigned to the slimeballs/crazymakers.

Extreme apprehension is often evident in the patient, as well as significantly involved family members. During the break one evening, Mark, the husband of Kim (a patient), asked me if I was going to be in his group later that evening. I told him "I don't know. I think Mary is planning to come in here tonight." Mark looked at Kim, Kim looked at Mark, and then they both looked at me...and their faces were pale! When I returned to the SED office, the counselors were interested in Mark's and Kim's responses. Mary laughed, but it sounded like the laugh of triumphant challenge. "Let's go" she said.

The following account was deemed as "wonderful work" by the entire staff of SED. It involved the clinical director challenging a patient, previously identified as a slimeball, to a ritualized game of adult red-rover.

Mary stood behind Mark (patient's husband) and pretended to be his voice. She addressed Kim (patient).

Mary: You Bitch. The more I come here, the sicker I see you are....I don't know why I put up with this shit. [Mike looked shocked. He sat straight in his chair and looked at his wife.] Do you want him?

Kim: Yes.

Mary: You'll have to fight for him.

[Mary then arranged a lineup of three of the biggest and strongest men and herself. They double linked their arms and wrists forming a human wall between Kim and her husband (who sits on a chair behind this human boundary). Again, Mary addressed Kim.]

Mary: You have to push your way through. Come on, come on you pussy...pussy, pussy, pussy.

Kim gave a reluctant push between Mary and Bob (a patient who weighed over 350 pounds.).

Mary: Oh, a ladylike pussy...come on slut, you bitch!

Kim: Shit [pushing harder].

Mary: Oh, shit [mimicking Kim but in simpering tone].

Kim: Goddamn [pushing].

Mary: Goddamn [mimicking Kim in simpering tone]. Next you'll say mother-fucker, pussy. Go on, you baby pussy...whore!...cunt!

[All the others watching this scene looked uncomfortable or shocked. Some had open mouths, others were averting their gaze.]

Kim: You want me to say "fuck."

Mary: You want me to say "fuck" said the pussy [mimicking Kim].

Kim: FUCK! [Screams Kim.] [And she then literally beat her way through Mary and Bob. Mary paused, then turned to the audience and held up her wrist with a broken watchband hanging from it.]

Mary: Look, she broke my watch—she really got tough. [She turned to Kim and told her to go to Mark and Mark stood up. They hugged. It appeared they were both shaking.]

Mary: It's so sweet. I want you to sit next to him—you deserve it...You fought for him tonight. [Mary then turned to Bob and the others.] I want you to take extra special care of Kim tonight because she might try to go back [to the way she was].

Even though the session was over, no one moved to leave the room. They all stood around looking at Mary as if they were in a trance—as if she had performed some form of incredible magic. Finally, a few began to speak, and then there was almost an uproar as those in the room left to share this event with their peers outside.

These punitive rituals of reformation are by far the most dramatic and stressful for everyone involved, including staff and other patients. Ironically, in some instances the slimeball/crazymaker appears to be almost unaffected by the event in comparison to her peers on SED. One patient noted that staff had assigned her a "coffin exercise" in order to release unexpressed feelings of rage and resentment toward her deceased aunt. She stated:

I had to dig my aunt back up and beat her up. I didn't feel that anger toward her anymore—so it really didn't work....You see, I did that once before—

opened the coffin and beat her up with batacas when I was in here....I was just too tired to do it again. I didn't feel that hatred...I had nothing to say to her...but it sure got to some of the others! They were balling like babies—and it was my aunt, not theirs!! Pretty weird, huh?

Another typical ritual assigned to the slimeballs/crazymakers is titled the "burial exercise." This ritual is used to help the patient express painful emotions that "have been buried" with the deceased. For this ritual one of the other patients is selected to represent the deceased significant other. This patient then lies on the floor as if she is dead and lying in a casket. Other patients represent significant family members or friends.

Initially Darlene was labeled as "a disgustingly slimy broad...a real slimeball." However, over the course of treatment she was identified as a "sickie...a crazymaker." This new label coincided with the disclosure of two prior suicide attempts as well as a family history of four suicides. Because Darlene had again talked about feeling suicidal in Ellen's group, this issue was addressed in staffing. It was decided by Mary that she would confront Darlene that evening because "she's wallowing in pain with an ace in the hole which is eating with the end result of suicide." Mary further commented:

> His suicide [Darlene's father] is a most glorious and worshipful thing [to her]—he jumped up and threw himself out of a window...so we need to have her yell and curse her father—[she needs to] bury him.

After group began, Mary asked Darlene if she had brought her plan concerning "your being released Friday—of what you are going to do." Darlene said she had completely forgotten her assignment and proceeded to present a list of differences between herself and her mother. Mary noted that her response was "crazy-making."

> Mary: You get others to work really hard for you and you stay out of it and then threaten to go and eat yourself into oblivion and then kill yourself...[Mary continued speaking.]...Barbara [Darlene's mother who was present in the room] said it was that you haven't dealt with your father's death [suicide]...*And* your grandfather, and two aunts who committed suicide, too.
>
> Barbara: People said he [her husband] was "Christ-like."
>
> Darlene: Yeah, he was.

Mary: ...Because in this family, you worship suicide, those who have killed themselves have been venerated...we're going to do a burial exercise. Who could represent your father?

Darlene: I'd like you, Rosemary, to be my dad. [She turned to Mary] Because she's soft and warm like my dad.

[Then Mary asks Darlene and Barbara to link arms and stand over "Dad" (Rosemary) and "tell him off."]

Barbara: [angry voice] You really made me so mad. You left me alone...with the kids—and the bills...

Darlene: [soft and droning voice] I miss you...you were so wonderful to me...you loved me and gave me just what I wanted...

[Mary physically separates Darlene and her mother, and then speaks to Barbara.]

Mary: You'll have to watch Darlene, now. Darlene's having a love affair with her father.

Mary: [turning to Darlene] Go ahead now and worship him. [Darlene immediately kneels down by her "Dad's" head. She leans over and cradles his head in her lap. She begins sobbing and cries out with a choking voice.]

Darlene: I don't want to be left behind, Daddy...I love you...I want to be with you Daddy...take me with you....

Two of the other patients were crying openly. Another patient became so distraught that she wanted to leave the room. Mary told her, "You are not to leave." This patient stood by the door sobbing. So I got up and put my arm around her and we watched the others.

Mary was standing next to Barbara, with her arm behind Darlene's mother's back as tears ran down Barbara's cheeks. Mary was also resting her head on Barbara's shoulder as they stood watching Darlene caress her "father's" face.

Then Darlene sat up abruptly and faced Mary. They talked about Darlene wanting to leave SED even if she would have to go AMA (Against Medical Advice). She did not want aftercare (outpatient therapy). Mary told her she might have to pay $10,000 herself if the insurance refused to pay because she was AMA. Darlene said,

That's OK. I just want to leave here as soon as possible. There is nothing here for me, I don't want to live in reality. It's too painful. I want to be with my father...

Mary then asked each person in the group to respond to Darlene. Everyone said they would be sad if she were to die.

Darlene: I don't know why you are *so* concerned about me...it makes me uncomfortable.

Mary: All these people love you...

Darlene: I'm sorry—but I still want to be with my father.

Rosemary: It's your legacy to be "Christlike" and sacrifice yourself—so your dad won't be seen as so bad for killing himself.

Sandy: Your dad wants you to live.

Darlene: My dad wants me to be happy and I'll be happier with him.

Several patients pleaded with Darlene to stay. Darlene was not influenced in the slightest. Finally, she said, "I'm not buying any of it...no matter what anyone says."

Barbara: All right then (angry voice) if that's what you really want to do—well, go ahead. See if it matters...not one bit.

Mary: [You] can't do that. She's [Darlene] the powerful one. You look strong, but Darlene's death would be devastating to you.

Barbara: I know.

Mary: So Darlene's got all the power. [Darlene just say there, staring at Mary and her mother for several minutes. It appeared as if the group was at a stalemate.]

Rosemary: I have this psychic ability—and when I played you dad, I felt a rush of energy into my shoulders and a voice say to me "Darlene, go on." I think he means to tell you to go on and live.

Darlene: That feels really good...I believe you Rosemary. And I wouldn't believe anyone else.

Rosemary: I'd never lie to you, that's why—and you *know* it.

Darlene: I do.

Mary: Well, why don't you write a dialogue with your father tonight and see if he tells you anything. Same thing goes for you three [three patients who had become so upset]. You know, Jackie, you are only a few steps behind her [Darlene]...I hope this has helped you, too.

[Everyone seemed very hesitant about leaving the room, and most remained seated in silence.]

Darlene: Well, I guess I'll leave first because no one will move.

Mary: Don't bother. Who do you think you are? You aren't that important. [And Mary left first.]

Once in the staff room, Mary called the psychiatrist to set up an appointment for Darlene. She also ordered the nursing staff to "watch her." A few minutes later I passed Darlene in the lounge. She was laughing and joking with several patients who had not been in our group. I expressed some surprise at how unaffected

Darlene appears considering how traumatic the past hour had been for the other group members, who had gone to their rooms for "reflection."

Mary: Well, what did you expect? She flips in and out so fast...the psychiatrist says she can't be committed to a psych ward because by the time she'd get there she wouldn't exhibit any symptoms...but he'll see her tomorrow.

Sandy: I didn't want to let her back in, after she left the first time. But the administrators got together before I got there and decided to let her back in...

Mary: I would never have let her in in the first place—she's so therapy wise...she says all the right things with no feelings—she's really crazy-making for staff.

In conclusion, specialized rituals of reformation are assigned to patients based on the unofficial patient labels that have previously been designated by staff. These rituals are designed to challenge the patient into assuming new means of expressing emotions that govern eating patterns. Staff hope that by challenging the patient's typical self-defeating mode of social interaction the patient will attain greater awareness and experience using an alternative means of expressing emotions.

Overall, reformation rituals are designed to transform the patient on an emotional level, using various behavioral change techniques as the primary means of motivation. Whether or not long-term or permanent change is actually achieved could not be ascertained. However, most of the reformation rituals do appear to have some initial (temporary) impact on the patient's consciousness, as well as causing increased stress for the other patients on the unit.

NORMALIZATION CEREMONIES

The third mechanism of social control utilized by the SED staff is the normalization ceremony. A normalization ceremony is composed of a series of three rituals conducted exclusively during the discharge stage of the patient's career. It consists of a final discharge staffing at the completion of inpatient treatment; the formal and informal announcements to family and peers of the patient's new status; and finally, a good-bye ceremony at the termination of aftercare treatment.

Prior to the beginning of a normalization ceremony, staff debate and carefully rehearse what specifically will be told to the patient during final staffing. Occasionally the clinical director explicitly directs the therapists "not to speak unless you have something positive to say" to the patient. In fact, in some dramatic instances, the clinical director reframes a patient's earlier negative behavior and redefines her lack of progress for the staff, in order to support this positive emphasis at the point of termination of inpatient status.

One such case involved an anorexic patient named Angie, previously labeled by staff as a slimeball/crazymaker. She had tried to commit suicide before entering the hospital and became so depressed while hospitalized that staff worried she might repeat her attempt. She did not, but what was intriguing was that the clinical director took this information about her background and behavior on the unit, and revised Angie's final evaluation that was planned by staff. The following describes how these events unfolded on SED.

A staff meeting was held ten days prior to Angie's discharge to aftercare status. She had been on the SED for seven weeks at this time, and the treatment team reported high frustration and disappointment at her lack of progress.

> Lisa: Angie's lost four pounds, and she's controlling her food.
> Jody: I feel like discharging her. I don't see any progress here, and neither does Mary. She needs to get into some pain out there [outside the hospital] or go to a psychiatric hospital if she is suicidal.
> Dr. C.: She is on antidepressant medication. She needs psychiatric care and anorexic care...she is an agitated depressive. I've worked with her for twice a week and I see her like the other of my patients in the hospital and she drains me. She may need long-term...my perfectionism smarts but some aren't helped as much as others...

One week later, during a staff meeting, members began discussing Angie's discharge and what they planned to tell her in her final staffing.

Jody: She was initially catatonic.

Mary: I see remarkable progress with her.

[Everyone on staff appears shocked that Mary insists there was remarkable progress for Angie.]

Sandy: What are you talking about? Angie?!?

Maggie: She's not really aware of her feelings at all—she concentrates it all on the food...

Mary: [turning to the director of nursing] I see remarkable progress, don't you, Shirley?

Shirley: Oh yes...she has a sense of humor—it's sarcastic—under that catatonic state—she's made progress here...really changed.

Sandy: But she's lost *four* pounds!! [Angie is a severely emaciated anorexic.]

Mary: Anybody say anything to her about it? [pause] No? Well, good! We don't want to emphasize that [weight] here....I really am pleased with Angie. Didn't someone say she was a miracle? [Mary turns to Shirley] I really think so....She's in a new breakthrough place—she needs a new therapist and I will recommend one for her in staffing. [There is a pause in the discussion. Some of the therapists make eye contact with each other.]

Sandy: She did come to see me and insisted she *asked* to work very insistently [in group]...

Doctor: Angie needs to hear positive stuff. But she takes it in and hears everything and brings it back.

Mary: Angie did come out with her feelings—but he [Angie's husband] is the one who refuses to move. She beat him with the bataca [in therapy] but he stood there rigid and told whole group told him he was fixed and the one who was *not* moving...Angie was flushed in the face and really worked and had energy. So I think it all revolved around him. He's the pivot point in the family. She's into progress and into recovery....I'm very pleased with her...and we're going to have her final staffing tomorrow, and I expect you to share this....I don't want anyone to speak who doesn't agree— no one is to talk if they don't believe it, either. I won't have anyone speaking for the group and being phony. Everyone understand? [All nodded.]

In every final staffing I attended, the staff present the same message of hope and recovery to the patient. Even when directed to chart information that can be constructed as negative, negativity is generally not acknowledged openly during this ritual. For example, Darlene, a crazymaker, was to be discharged in two days "because it's twenty-eight days on Friday and her insurance is running out." The therapist who was charting her record was instructed to "write discharge for insurance reasons—she's not doing well...[you] let us know by Thursday if she can pay it [herself] because insurance is over on Friday and we'll have to let her go even though we don't thing she's ready."

However, when Darlene attended her final staffing on Friday (she could not afford to pay for continued hospitalization), she was not clearly informed of the staff's reluctance to release her. In fact, she received a final staffing that was similar to that of her peers. Ultimately, the labels and procedures stemming from the macrostructure of insurance and legislation prove more significant than the micro-politics at SED.

Normalization ceremonies are designed to acclimate the patient to her new role of recovered compulsive overeater prior to leaving the inpatient and aftercare programs. The first of these three events is a rigidly structured meeting in which the paraprofessional and professional staff, who have certified patients as compulsive overeaters, then certify the patients as recovered. This final formal "staffing" procedure is performed in one of the therapy group rooms, in which the therapists are again seated in a semicircle with a chair in the center for the soon-to-be-pronounced-recovered patient. Silence is strictly maintained before the patient enters the room and is told to sit in the chair. The patient is again informed she must not speak or ask questions. She is only permitted to listen. The staff members then singly address the patient, stating *only* the positive attributes of the patient and her remarkable progress of recovery. After this, one spokesperson for the group gives the final summation and informs the patient that she will be moving into the aftercare group. The appointed spokesperson is usually the clinical director or the primary therapist assigned to the patient. The spokesperson also is expected to begin the ceremony speaking first. Others follow in a ritualized order, until all who wish to have spoken. The patient is then told to leave the room and the staff applaud as she leaves.

What follows is a detailed account of a final staffing:

> [Bev came in and took her seat facing the therapists.]
> Sandy: We are going to discharge you tomorrow. [Bev looked stunned.]
> Maggie;   I know this was a surprise—but you look shocked.
> Bev: I am, I...
> Jody: No, Bev, you can't speak now.
> Sandy: I am really going to miss you a whole lot. You've done so well. [Sandy has tears in her eyes.]

Ellen: I'm looking forward to having you in family group as an outpatient.

Maggie: I'm really glad you are an outpatient now because you have to talk.

Sandy: You have changed so much since you have been here. You are ready now to go out and deal with your issues. You know what they are and can talk about them and I'm really happy for you.

Jody: We think you are ready to go out and we would support you continuing to explore and grow.

Sandy: We want to encourage you to work your program and to get to meetings. You know what to do now. You are ready to leave.

Ellen: And I'd just like to encourage you to jump right into OA work now—it's time for you and it's very important that you do this for yourself.

Sandy: You have made such progress....I was so pleased when you talked about perfection for you today...before you leave, we want you to have some time to pitch at meetings about your feelings...about feeling a failure and not being perfect. That's it...so you'll leave after education tomorrow at three. Go home and go out to eat with your husband and family. And then, come back for aftercare.

The therapists all began clapping for her. Bev jumped up and turned at the door, "Thank you so much—and I love you all!" Then she left the room looking very happy. Screams and laughter were heard from the hall after the door was closed. Some of Bev's peers had been waiting for her to come out of staffing and share her good news with them.

Meanwhile, in the staff meeting, the counselors continued to discuss Bev in very glowing terms. They shared, among themselves, how deeply rewarding this ritual was for all concerned and commented how much they had personally enjoyed this particular staffing.

Ellen: I really hate to see her go. Do we have to let her? Did you see her face—she's so soft. [Ellen held her hands to the sides of her face.]

Sandy: I know. But I'm so proud of myself. I didn't even cry. I'm growing up. [Sandy's eyes look very watery and her nose is a deep pink.]

Maggie: She's a real doll...we'll all miss her.

Although I felt skeptical about the intense degree of emotional involvement displayed by staff, attachment and positive feelings are unanimously expressed for all patients. However, staff's elevated positive emotional arousal is temporary, and in some cases, extremely brief. Usually, staff and the patient maintain a period of euphoria for one to two days. After this period, emotions return to the status quo on the unit.

The second normalization ritual involves formal and informal announcements to the other patients and family members. The patient usually leaves the final staffing in shocked surprise, and is met outside the door by her peers who hear the clapping of the staff. The patient then informs them of her new status, which is followed by shouting, screams of laughter and general glee and hugging. Late the same evening, a staff member, during the family therapy and educational meetings, announces to the other patients and family members the patient's new status.

Ellen made this announcement during the education session:

> Everyone, I have some wonderful news to announce [general applause and laughter]. Most of you have already heard that Cathy was staffed today [loud cheering], and we [staff] unanimously decided that she is ready to move into aftercare [boisterous cheers and clapping]. We are all so proud of you, Cathy. [Ellen looked at Cathy and smiled broadly.] You are a real miracle of recovery [more applause]. And we all know you can do it...one day at a time!

Congratulations are extended during the therapy groups, with everyone hugging the patient at the end of the group and wishing her well. During this time, it is common practice for other patients who have achieved aftercare status to give advice and encouragement to the patient. In addition, they frequently exchange telephone numbers in order to provide additional mutual support.

SED provides six weeks of aftercare treatment, occurring between the second and third normalization ceremonies. In stark contrast to the optimism of the final staffing, during aftercare the patient is continuously bombarded with messages concerning the delicate fragility of her recovery. Sermons are used by the staff to remind the patient of the dire consequences of "leaving the program without commitment." One staff member noted,

> I feel extremely fortunate, because not all of us manage to stay in control. Elaine, for instance, she's been as thin as a post when she left seven months ago, has doubled her size—eating again, unable to stop, and proving to me that compulsive overeating, like alcoholism, is something that can be

controlled—day by day—but never cured....helped by the good example of the staff and all those recovered overeaters who have left and kept working their program [and the fear of having a relapse like Elaine] keeps me coming to meetings. Somehow those OA meetings keep me safe and happy and shapely— and that, to me, is certainly worth whatever time I spend at them....I have to keep working my program or I will die, just like I almost did before....

The patient is again indoctrinated with information that her recovery is only a temporary respite from a progressively lethal disease, which is conditional upon the "maintenance of a fit spiritual condition." She is taught that she is "recovered" but not cured, nor should she ever hope to be. At this point of release from the institution, not one patient views herself as having been cured of her affliction. Rather, she proudly asserts that she is a "recovering" compulsive overeater or "in the process of getting better." The staff generally fulfilled their mission of convincing the patient to reinterpret her past, present, and future behavior in terms of the medical/disease model. The staff successfully bring the patient to accept a perpetually needy state, in which she must maintain dependency on an external program for support and recovery. (Staff regularly attend OA meetings as participants.) This strategy is similar to one of the conclusions in Laslett and Warren's article (1975, p. 78) that states, "Successful behavior change...may require lifetime organizational membership..." in order for an obese person to maintain "Normal behavior and a normal way of life" (p. 79).

The third ritual is the final good-bye ceremony held at the end of aftercare treatment. At the beginning of the educational group, the teaching therapist announces that it is the patient's last night of treatment. She then gives the patient permission to address the staff, patients and family members. The patient proceeds to the front of the room. She acknowledges her new status as a "recovering compulsive overeater," and tells an abbreviated luminary saga concerning her recovery. For example, a very large woman moved to the front of the room and faced her audience. She proceeded to tell the audience this story.

I'm Bernie, and I'm a compulsive overeater. I called [the unit] desperate [for help]. I couldn't stop eating candy....Baby Ruths, and I'm a diabetic. I called here and they said, "make a decision—it's your life..." I came...

> I had always run my own life but I learned discipline here. These tiny women [counselors] really have the answers. I wanted to kill myself many times before—but now, I can go out and live and eat and *think*!....Do your first step right away—do what they tell you...God, bless you Mary, you saved my life. When I wake, I say, "God, thank you for my abstinence," like they taught me in maintenance [aftercare] on Saturday..."

In another instance, an anorexic patient created a similar luminary saga at the point of her final discharge ceremony. Angela walked quickly to the front and spoke very softly to the audience.

> Hello, I'm Angela, and I am a compulsive overeater....I think I would have died if it hadn't been for this program....I honestly wanted to die, I just didn't seem to be able to do it. This program has saved my life and my marriage. My husband was sick of watching me and trying to get me to eat. And now we both have a program of recovery. He goes to meetings and I go to meetings...and sometimes it is tough. But we will make it. And I've learned to trust my Higher Power....Thank you everyone.

This event is frequently a highly emotional experience, not only for the patient who is likely to cry, but also for her peers and the staff she's leaving behind.. After this emotional moment, there is applause by the staff and patients. Some also shout out words of encouragement, such as "Keep coming back," "You're never alone," or "Hang in there," as the patient returns to her seat. At times, all of the members of her group also tell her how much she will be missed and proceed to give her advice on how to continue to work her program outside of the hospital.

Normalization ceremonies are viewed by staff and patients as the completion of the patient's "rite of passage." They represent a change in social status from "sick" to "recovering." This last phase of reaggregation is a graduation celebration. This is the moment they have strived for together throughout treatment. The ultimate goal of treatment has been successfully reached at the pronouncement of the patient's termination of treatment.

While there is a normalization ceremony for patients who depart through appropriate channels, those patients who do not follow this path receive different treatment. For example, policy formally states that if a patient is "not working" the program, she will be asked to leave in a formal staffing meeting. However, in real life on the unit when a patient does not meet staff's expectations, she usually leaves of her own accord. Then there is no formal staffing, no announcement and no good-bye ceremony. This type of termination is a traumatic event for both the patient and the staff. Because the staff are highly invested in patient recovery, they are usually very upset when a patient leaves AMA (against medical advice). Below is a brief excerpt from a staff meeting:

> Maggie: What happened to June?
> Alice: Roy [husband] told her she had to decide to leave or stay within twenty minutes on Saturday morning, because this isn't a Christian group. She left.
> Mary: Do you think she'll come back?
> Sandy: No.
> Mary: Then she'll kill herself.
> Ruth
> [administrator]: If anyone [counselors] was here, do you think you could have helped him or her?
> Sandy: Yes, if we had been here, we could stop them. It's an extremely sick relationship, they feed off one another.
> Lisa: No indication that this would happen.
> Alice: Well, he's a practicing alcoholic [by his own admission in group] in denial—it doesn't surprise me.
> Ellen: [after discussion had finished] I'll call her in Dallas and see if they got home safely.

It was evident that while there was a failure on the part of staff to integrate these two into the hospital coterie, the staff did not assume responsibility but proceeded to blame the patient and her husband. They also made dire predictions about the patient's future without the SED's particular mode of treatment and recovery.

The methods by which the staff relate to the SED patients and determine their treatment and how they attempt to maintain control over the patients' responses to treatment are intimately connected to and dependent on an ongoing informal labeling process. In turn this typification process is used as an explanation for a patient's progress or lack of improvement (recovery) in treatment.

The staff use various mechanisms of social control to impart the knowledge, norms and attitudes of the SED program. The liminality of hospitalization provides numerous rituals to humble and discipline the patient. These rites function to restructure the identity of the patient in which she accepts a permanently stigmatized identity while normalizing her behavior, her way of life, and possibly (over time) even her physical appearance.

Chapter VI

Storytelling

The SED patients use storytelling as the well-socialized response to the various labels and mechanisms of control used by the staff. Newcomers, patients in the liminal phase, and those ready for discharge tell stories that coincide with their stage of "recovery." Storytelling is the mechanism for reconstruction of the patient's biography. The patient eventually constructs a bad, old self which becomes transformed into a new, recovered self. In turn, staff analyze stroytelling to determine the extent to which a patient is "recovered" or not recovered."

There are many additional functions of storytelling reported in the sociological and anthropological literatures that apply to SED. Some of the most common ones include aiding in the education of the "young" (Toelken, 1979); promoting a group's feeling of solidarity (Passin and Bennett 1943); providing socially sanctioned ways for individuals to act toward others (Messenger 1959); serving as a vehicle for social protest (Wang 1935); offering an enjoyable escape from reality (Tolken 1979); and converting dull work into play (Dundes 1971).

Although the universal theme of the stories on SED revolves around the eating disorder and its effects on the patient, there are three distinct types of stories that parallel the stages of recovery: tormented tales of the painful past (newcomer); horror stories of the unengaged (liminal patient); and luminary sagas (patient at discharge). The form of the stories is commonly associated with the following format: first, the patient exposes herself via painful events of the past; then, she reveals her current experience and emotions (whether positive or negative); and finally, she expresses the moral or "the lesson" for the story. (The lesson might be in an overt or covert message to the audience.) This universality is an essential characteristic of storytelling on the eating disorder unit, matching the universality of staff ideology. Most storytellers begin by sharing painful events.

> I am an alcoholic and a compulsive overeater, and for awhile, I was anorexic. I wouldn't eat....I remember my mother and my friend trying to help me, but it wouldn't work because I thought my mom was trying to sabotage me, and I didn't care about my friend....I would lay there and measure my bones with my fingers. I saw myself in the mirror and thought I was fat. But I can remember one time I looked, and I saw an old lady of 99 who was all shrunken over and very emaciated with flabby skin all over—and it was me! But I couldn't believe it....

After assigning a storytelling ritual, staff usually offers some overt sympathetic communication such as "feelings are painful" or "the past is very painful" but it is necessary that it be shared. However, there is always the covert message that if it is not shared with the group, the patient will not completely recover. Even if the patient does not wish voluntarily to share about the past, she does so in order to obtain the benefit of recovery.

Storytelling mirrors familiar or common situations from everyday life. But the unusual, or even the seemingly impossible, is an important entertaining ingredient in each type of story. Overwhelmingly, the most tragic, dramatic, humorous or heroic stories on SED receive the greatest response from the staff. In fact, the more emotionally arousing the story, the more likely it is to be repeated in detail during staff meetings for therapeutic analysis and retold in educational groups for the new patients' benefit. The importance of the entertainment function was commented upon by staff as well as patients. For example, a listening patient rolled her eyes and sighed deeply, and the storytelling patient said, "I'm doing it again...I'm boring everyone." While in another instance, a staff member remarked, "She really gets to me, her stories are so dramatic!"

It is often because the patient is seeking approval from staff and peers that she enhances the style of presentation by exaggeration or greater personal self-disclosure than would be appropriate in other social circumstances. In SED, if a patient tells an unusually moving story, she receives greater encouragement from peers and the staff. Others are more likely to talk to the patient—to comment on how they were touched by the story or to offer some advice. It appears that there is a great deal of support when a patient talks about how difficult it is to live outside of the hospital and to continue to work a good recovery program. Others frequently encourage the storyteller "to keep sharing." There are also comments such as "I feel closer to you because you shared about being [afraid, disappointed, hurt, angry]."

Self-disclosure through storytelling is the major means of gaining approval on SED. Staff sayings, such as "We are as sick as we are secret," encourage patients to share personal feelings and thoughts. However, there could be some negative consequences to self-disclosure. For example, an explosive patient stated the following: "After I did my First Step, I told my husband that I was fed up and angry, and I wanted to leave [the unit]. And he got scared and left!" This was proof to her that revealing feelings was dangerous. However, she received a lot of attention and encouragement from the staff and her peers to remain. She stayed.

Storytelling also plays a major role in education, particularly of the newcomer and unengaged. The importance of storytelling as a pedagogic device is documented by the many morals or lessons found in the tales themselves. Stories incorporating morals are introduced to inculcate general attitudes and principles: such as *awareness* of one's "disease" and of grandiose desires to be perfect; urgings toward *acceptance* of one's and other's imperfections; and *action* "working for recovery" or "we strive for progress—not perfection." Morals are also introduced to ridicule self-pity, rebelliousness, and denial.

> We aren't like other people. We are different. We can't stop eating once we start. You have to be honest. That's why I told everyone about my slip [overeating] a few months ago. *We are not perfect.* You need to know that and not beat yourself...the natural tendency is to deny—that it's not that bad! We want to believe we can relax, and it's so easy like the rollers in the spas are beating off the fat! If you could have—you would have changed. This is the hardest thing you'll do in your entire life.

Storytelling is used to express potential threat (i.e., relapse), to direct another's behavior unobtrusively, or to encourage a person toward some action. When a patient "acts out" foolishly or rebelliously, she usually hears her actions commented upon in a horror story. "She still hasn't learned yet to clear away the junk. She had no awareness of her disease and the wreckage of her past."

Staff storytelling is employed against individuals who attempt to deviate from social conventions on the unit. Often, staff horror stories are used both to express social approval of those who conform and to express disapproval of those who do not. Horror stories are also employed to control, influence, and direct the activities of patients and family members. In addition, these accounts become an internalized check on behavior for patients. Thus, stories of this type serve as instruments both for self-control and for the control of others.

Instruction in the stories is often implicit: "The group is necessary for you to see where you are and to gain an awareness of what you are going through." Or stories speak directly: "You can't be sure of who you are—only when you are clean of the addictive cycle can we see who you really are." Instructive criticism as a form of social control is seen by staff as an important means of censuring misbehavior.

Information in the stories in highly respected in its own right. Its teaching is regarded as important and it contains practical rules for the guidance of those who wish to recover. Stories are also used in the disciplining of a new patient. For example, staff members used patient stories "to keep them (patients) directed, instead of lots of new topics and chaos." "They can identify with the problem because their own problems are seen as similar." The patients' initial attempt at storytelling occurs within the first or second week after hospitalization. These stories are sad and touching accounts of the newcomer's background.

TORMENTED TALES OF THE PAINFUL PAST

In general, tormented tales are taken from the mandatory First Step assignments that are read aloud to the staff and patients during therapy. I labeled these "tormented tales" because they consist almost entirely of extremely painful experiences from the storyteller's past.

When patients first tell their tales, there is often competition between participants in terms of the stigma of their eating disorder.

It typically appears in the form of the "I suffered most" syndrome. The stigma is thus transformed into an asset or achievement by its past tense. For example, as one patient began her tormented tale with the words, "I've been suffering for twenty years with this disease..." the patient besides me suddenly leaned over and whispered loudly to her friend, "Well, it's been even longer for me, starting when I was a child of three!"

According to Langness and Frank (1985, p. 109), two anthropologists who study life stories from various perspectives,

> If memory is selective, then there must be a prior structure of personal identity that provides the template by which certain events are cast as images significant enough to be stored.

The stored images from the patient's memory, which are selectively recalled in the tormented tales, were composed from historical material related to the social history and the medical history of the newcomer.

Social History

Social histories almost universally develop around the reporting of an unhappy childhood. There are several dimensions involved in the usual report of family life when growing up. The patient sees the affective/emotional climate as either chaotic or inappropriate. It is frequently either extremely volatile or very barren.

> I had a very unhappy childhood. I wasn't allowed to hate or even dislike my stepfather...I got a lot of motivation to be an excellent student. It was like they had a foot in my back pushing me...and that motivated me, but I depended on the external push. When they didn't, I collapsed, and I'd [over] eat. Either there was too much emotion or very little...I never knew what to expect when I'd get home [from school].

In addition, a significant or critical event is reported by every patient as affecting their development. In many cases, the child assumes the caretaker role and dependency of a parent occurs frequently in these stories.

> My father walked out on us when I was 13 years old...I was the oldest, and I just fell into the role of mother's helper....I never had any time to myself.

According to these patients, parents' verbalization of inner feelings is minimal or dramatically over-exaggerated, and incidents of abuse and/or neglect in childhood are not uncommon. In almost all the stories, there is a recounting of comparable problems to the eating disorder in the patient's family of origin.

> My dad used to beat me regular....He'd never say nothing....He'd come home and start in and sometimes I'd pass out. It was when he came home drunk, I hated it.

After the customary comments about their painful and frequently traumatic upbringing, patients are likely to discuss their current hurtful affiliations. They confess being dissatisfied in relationships, "blocking" emotions, "using" food; they disclose the ways in which they have ineffectively dealt with threatened or actual loss.

Dissatisfaction in relationships is a theme covering a wide range of situations . Patients usually include friends, family, significant others such as spouse or lover, and careers.

> I didn't have good relationships with women or men. I'd cross the street rather than say hello to those I wanted in my life....

> No matter what I do, I think people just want to be my friend because of what I did in the Olympics. I hate to go to the gym. I hate to go out with my friends. I'm sick of myself and my body....I feel so fat. [She is approximately 10-15 pounds overweight.]

> I felt like a victim. They were always doing it to me...mean and rotten....I couldn't see anything but that I was a victim....

> The job was awful. They were going bankrupt, and I'd stay out of fear of losing a job!

> My mother was very perfectionistic....I never did anything right. My husband is a recovered alcoholic, but he's so passive...he just sits...he won't talk. We haven't had sex in ten years. I think I married my father...

Blocking of emotions (in these stories) leads to compulsive behavior ranging from overeating to workaholism. The respondents report that the stifling of one emotion leads to not experiencing any emotions. The staff commonly refer to those individuals who experience this phenomenon as "feeling blockers." Staff is extremely pleased when a patient interprets "blocking" emotions as no longer acceptable and appears willing to express "those ugly feelings I've been stuffing down." Some of the patients' insights are reported to staff during therapy sessions. For example:

> When I hold one feeling down, it makes me hold down other feelings. I become so blocked that I'm really ineffectual in my life and work. I don't like myself, and that self loathing leads to food.

> Sometimes I'm really brittle. Sometimes I'm like a child. I'd say don't bother me with these big people things [work]—just leave me alone to get along. If you really knew who I was, you wouldn't like me.

> You [to deceased husband] really made me so mad! You left me alone...and the bills...so many bills....What else was there for me to do? I wasn't supposed to be mad at you. You couldn't help dying like that [cancer]...so I went numb, and I ate and ate, every night.

Langness and Frank (1985 p. 116) note that researchers doing fieldwork

> ...must take into consideration the particular rules of the social context in which the individual lives. This context and these rules become the background for understanding the choices that the individual makes.

The choices and interpretations that patients make are necessary for survival on SED, in addition to giving new meaning to their lives. In other words, stories have learned elements. For example, food is redefined by the hospital staff for the patients as a drug. Patients are socialized to believe it is "our drug of choice." In their stories, patients state that they most frequently "use" food to numb the pain they are experiencing. But, according to staff, patients can also use food as a reward, rebellion, or escape.

> Food was everything to me. I'd get it as a reward for being good. My mom would day, I'll buy you a candy bar if you'll just sit still for the doctor. Or, food was punishment if I was bad. She'd say, "You won't get any dessert if you kids don't stop fighting. They [parents] used it to make me guilty. "Think of all the starving children in China." There were threats if I didn't

eat everything on my plate...and, of course, food was good medicine. My mom would say, "A bowl of ice cream would cure anything."

When the environment was out of control, I tried to control my food. I'd go on a diet. I'd feel really secure. At least I'm controlling something in my life...I'd count my string beans...I was thinking about food all the time, but I couldn't eat it. And no matter what they said, they couldn't make me eat [anorexic].

I overheard one extremely obese male patient tell a therapist:

If I leave here before my time, I will be dead in a year. There is nothing else. This is the end of the line for me...compulsive people have to be very careful with what they use.

Many patients tell stories that interpret eating as the result of anxiety due to threatened or actual loss. They report using food as their outlet for their anxiety and frustration. Many have struggled with their problems for a considerable period of time. For example, a flight attendant from a major airline came to the clinic:

Because I'd lose my job if I don't weigh in at my goal weight. I'm on probation right now. I've been a stewardess for 15 years and for the last 10, I've had a weight problem, and it's hell.

Other respondent's tales likewise concern using food to deal with stress:

John threatened to divorce me if I didn't lose weight. I did. But then he went ahead anyway and got the divorce, and I started eating again.

My dad had a heart attack when I was little. So my mother always told me I had to be a good girl and not upset my father. And I really believed it was my responsibility to prevent his having another attack. I was a good girl, but I started eating then. Sometimes when I look back, I think they were sicker than I was!

Along with the social histories that cover the family of origin and their current network of family and friends, patients also incorporate into their tormented tales information dealing with their medical histories. Staff encourage patients to give a brief "medical report" of the medical consequences of their compulsive behavior. Staff are of the opinion that such a practice may help the patients more quickly "recognize the extent of their disease."

Medical History

The elements of a medical history include physical symptoms, prior chemical abuse and psychiatric dysfunctions. The patients recount physical symptomatology due to the eating disorder, and the resulting effects on their physical health. The symptoms and their effects are usually reported in a very graphic manner.

> I almost died three times....One time my sister said she couldn't stand it anymore and took me to the hospital. The doctors told me if I'd have waited, I'd have been dead. I had no potassium at all...really low electrolytes.

> I had my stomach stapled twice...I've been a vomiter for the past three years...on and off I do it, I guess.

> I had 10-50 pound weight fluctuations. I'd get up to a size 16, and then I'd diet and get the weight off and put it back on again...the doctors say my metabolism is shot....It will never be normal.

> I guess I developed my diabetes because I couldn't stay away from the sugar, anyway, that's what the doctor said.

The patients also elaborate on their chemical abuse history. These stories range from using diet pills and stimulants like caffeine to major tranquilizers, antidepressants, and street drugs.

> My drug of choice was Excedrin. I'd take two or three in the morning....It wasn't until later that I found out it had caffeine in it.

> I used to have about six drinks a day and take marijuna a couple times a week. I used to make $100-$200 for dealing to support my habit.

> Like a good overeater, alcoholic and addict, I took pills, drank and took shots in my fat ass from my husband who loved giving it to me in the ass because he liked to give me pain.

> I'd hide Vivarin and laxatives in the bathroom...I got down to 95 pounds and kept losing.

> I've tried every diet and every diet pill and shot that's been created. I would be so wired up, I couldn't sit still...Other times, I'd cry myself to sleep at night because I'd be on depressants...it was hell!

The most common component of these medical histories is developing compulsive patterns. Patients frequently report on their continuing obsession with food and other susbstances. They are also likely to relate stories of their various compulsions framed in the covert message that they suffer from a "disease." Compulsive patterns include such categories as binging, vomiting, compulsive work habits, spending, gambling, drugs, and sex. Also patients report related problems of depression and a history of suicidal attempts or suicidal ideation.

> Food stopped working for me...booze stopped working...and no matter what I did, the pain didn't go away....

> I was depressed all the time. In public, I'd be silent or quiet, but around friends and family, I'd be depressed.

> I tried to kill myself [once] before...it took the police three days to find me....I guess I'm glad now they did...I just couldn't take it anymore....

> I'd eat from the trash...eat it even if my husband threw in cigarette butts on the food. I'd dig it out and scrape off the butts and eat it.

While newcomers tell tormented tales of the painful past, patients that are well into the liminal stage, often hear stories about those that are struggling or unsuccessful with "working their program." These accounts are the SED "horror stories."

HORROR STORIES OF THE UNENGAGED

Horror stories are similar to tormented tales in that the accounts are usually very painful and dramatic. I labeled these stories of the unengaged because these are stories told by or about patients or persons who are not actively in recovering. Often, a newly admitted patient's family tells a horror story about the patient in their First Step assignment. On other occasions, staff share appalling accounts about former patients or those patients considered by staff to be disengaged from the program of recovery. The unengaged are seen as sufferers who have never been involved on the unit or persons who have failed to "work their programs," some even leaving the unit entirely to resume their compulsive behavior patterns.

Horror stories help maintain conformity to the accepted patterns of behavior on SED. More than simply serving to validate or justify institutions, beliefs and attitudes, these stories frequently serve as a means of applying social pressure and exercising social control.

The most frequently recounted horror stories by staff concern extremely obese patients. These stories are told as a means to reinforce for patients the importance of adherence to staff ideology. For example, a staff member told her group during therapy:

> I know a man who weights 585 pounds, and he actually had to shovel the garbage out of his room with a shovel! He'd bring in a bag of food and eat it and never take the wrappers or trash out....

Another staff member reported on a 350-pound woman who had entered into treatment and then left against medical advice:

> She was drinking 12 Pepsi's a day. We told her to expect sugar withdrawal. She couldn't take it and left [unit] craving sugar but denying it.

The majority of staff horror stories directly involve eating. In some cases, however, a staff member will relate abusive instances that happen to patients "who aren't into their recovery"; implying that the social response they receive is somehow their "own fault."

> There's a woman I know who has been married for 20 years and hasn't had any sex for 10 years. He calls her a pig or ignores her...I don't know, he may be impotent.

> Her brothers used to always call her whale and pig, ya know. He's addicted to everything...food, PCP, fucking...every which way...three, four or five people at a time just crazy...he lives in a hole...there are rats in the kitchen, but he's not poor! He'd throw a wrapper on the floor and it would sit there for a week....

On occasion, participants tell unengaged stories about themselves. These are patients who feel themselves to be, or actually are considered by staff to be, marginal patients. They are very likely to preface their appalling account with "I haven't been working my program very well" or "I'm not into my recovery." They are also likely to end their story with some kind of self-revelation statement such as, "I'm into the problem and not into the solution" or "I've got a lot to work on, huh?"

The following excert is from the First Step assignment of a mother of a newly admitted patient. According to staff, this mother "is still into the problem—not into the solution," because "she is too caught up in her daughter's drama...she needs to let go of her daughter A.S.A.P. [As Soon As Possible]." This mother declared:

> I can't stand to think about my daughter's marriage. It's so horrible. All she does is eat and drink. On Thanksgiving, she was passed out drunk on the bed, and her husband came home and kicked her and beat her up. I had to take her to the hospital....She swore she needed help, but she wouldn't get any. So now she's withdrawing....I've tried to help her and tell her what to do, but she doesn't want my help. It really gets to me. It hurts me a lot to see her in pain, but I guess I have to give her up....

While most stories convey lessons that are acceptable to and formally sanctioned by staff, patient and family member storytelling does not always endorse the SED philosophy. Sometimes, patients tell stories with socially unapproved messages. These messages deny the universality of the patient's status and locate the blame on external forces. Types of blame avoidance include: externalizing the problem, "She seems to put everything outside onto her mom and dad"; shifting the focus, "Instead of talking about herself, she got into storytelling about her son"; asking for assistance from significant others; or "getting to" the spouse by using others for pressuring.

> People tell me I look good, but I feel awful. I don't know what to do. Sometimes I want to talk and sometimes I don't. I feel crazy and want him [husband] to answer and tell me what to do.
>
> Counselor: [talking to husband] ...and that hooks you in as a co-compulsive overeater for her. You don't want to see her be self-destructive, but she sets you up to have all the answers and you don't. So she'll resent you and start eating....Let her tell her own story, okay?

Family members also tell blame-avoidance stories. In many instances they initially do not believe that they contribute to or reinforce the patient's behavior. They deny needing any personal assistance. It is the *patient* who has the problem—not them. And so the family members are requested by the staff to re-tell their stories in another "First Step." In fact, patients as well as family members may have to write and tell several versions of their "First Step" assignment, until staff decides "you finally got it right this time."

In addition, staff characterizes the lack of negative storytelling as "denial":

> She tries to portray this good American family. She is not as happy as she says in her stories

While others refuse to acknowledge any feelings:

> I don't let myself know what my feelings are so I don't have to make decisions or have an opinion or take any action.

The response of the counselors is that

> It is a natural tendency to deny pain. To say it's not that bad....So sometimes the stories sound like fairy tales. We let them tell their stories— but when we hear stuff that doesn't fit—doesn't ring true—well, we remember. And we call them on it later...And maybe they'll have to rewrite their First Step.

Attempting to conform to SED ideology and gain staff approval by false presentation, extreme exaggeration, or obvious manipulation produces the opposite effect from that which is sought. On one occasion, the clinical staff discussed a "manipulative anorexic" with the patients and families. A staff member stated that this patient's recovery was impeded because she was receiving a great deal of attention for inappropriate behaviors and stories that gave the erroneous impression that she was extremely fragile. Another staff member noted, "She gets a lot of attention from everyone. She's manipulating you into feeling afraid she'll break—you need to see she's not fragile— she's strong!" Thus, staff approval is conditionally based on the perceived honesty of the patient, as well as the amount of self-disclosure.

LUMINARY SAGAS

The climax of all storytelling is the final "good-bye" in the form of a luminary saga during the normalization ceremony process. Luminary sagas, for the most part, are opposite to the horror stories of the unengaged. These are not the accounts of the old, fat, nonprogram person, but of the new, recovered, programmed self. These sagas are told to encourage those who are still struggling with their eating disorder. "What we do is share our experience, strength and hope," reported one staff member, and by implication establish staff's universalizing ideology as correct. Thus, sagas serve as a reminder to the storyteller of where she comes from and how without the help of the recovery program, she can easily return to compulsive behavior. I named these particular stories luminary sagas because they essentially are narratives of heroic exploits which inspire the listener.

In addition to expounding program ideology, staff use their personal sagas as a means to dispel myths. When a staff member displayed her bruised arm and told the group about fighting with her husband, she said "Here is progress." Her progress was that she didn't continue to badger him or he to hit her. One of the other family members in the group said he was "shocked." He then stated, "You've been in the OA program for so long. I thought your marriage was perfect." Her response was "No marriage is perfect...that's only in fairy tales."

Storytelling provides the opportunities for the storyteller to share her successes in the program. This serves to provide the participants, and especially the newcomers to the unit, with hopeful expectancy. The wisdom and pleasure of recovery is thus passed on to newcomers. It is not presented as absolute wisdom, but wisdom that is relative to specific situations, which explains why there are stories recommending opposite courses of action. For example, one storyteller might say, "Let go and let God [handle it]," and at another point in the story she would suggest, "You have to do the footwork. God isn't going to do it for you."

Basically, sagas are told about overlapping areas of recovery: physical progress, emotional health, and spiritual development. During the discharge phase, at the point where the patient is being reintegrated into society, these sagas serve to validate the staff assessment that the patient has "recovered." These three signs of recovery are seen as based on the redirection of negative inner feelings that previously have "inevitably" precipitated a binge or some type of dysfunctional eating behavior. These patients have demonstrated successful emotion management. Clear demonstration of these signs of progress in treatment contribute to the staff's impression that the patient has "recovered."

Storytelling justifies SED rituals and institutions for those who perform and observe them. The luminary saga is used to testify to the program's success. As stated by a woman who dropped from 230 pounds to 169 pounds, "It's changed my life. You've heard my story...and [began sobbing] you [collectively] helped save my life! One day at a time, I work my program—and I live!"

Thus, storytelling serves an indispensable function: it expresses, enhances and codifies belief. It also contains practical rules for patient's guidance. Storytelling strengthens one's program of recovery and endows it with a greater value and prestige. Storytelling is, therefore, a vauable means of self-reinforcement.

One patient succinctly stated her belief and dependency on the recovery program:

> I'd have to go against my parent's messages, who I used for my validation. I'm not dependent on them now. I know I'm not like other people. I can't stop binging once I start. Yes, I am a compulsive overeater, and I can't control my own life. But I have help from my Higher Power and the program. I depend on that to live...and I'm recovering one day at a time.

By means of luminary sagas, storytellers show how the freedom from binging, vomiting, or starving has brought about a radical improvement in their physical health. These luminary sagas are hero stories. They are usually full of adventures and achievements of an extraordinary kind (overcoming death by chronic illnesses, tremendous weight loss, kicking an ancillary drug addiction).

> I used to eat chocolate and toast—a gallon of chocolate and a loaf of toast. I never ate one piece of toast in my life. Then I got into my recovery, and I found my meals getting smaller and smaller. I was over 250 pounds, and now I'm 178 pounds.

An alumnia at the annual Christmas part was asked to share "her story" with the patients. She recalled:

> I came in [to recovery program] at over 200 pounds. I went from a size 24-1/2 to a size 5, where I am now. And I never thought it would happen to me. And I stopped taking pills...I would gulp down 3 or 4 at a time but no more!

> I called desperate. I couldn't stop eating candy and I'm a diabetic. I wanted to kill myself many times before, but I can go out and live and eat and think!

An important aspect of emotional health is the avoidance of abusing food in the face of difficulty.

> Being a successful abstainer means that I abstain no matter what. I have to be willing to go through what I have to, in order to recover. If I get sloppy, I don't have to eat a supermarket. I just have to be honest with myself.

In these luminary sagas, patients report that although severe stress originated from external sources, they were able to overcome all obstacles to abstaining from compulsive overeating.

> My husband and I went out for coffee three weeks ago, and I thought he was going to tell me everything was going to be alright now that I'm out of the hospital. But he didn't. He told me he wanted a divorce. He's left—not just me and our son—he left the state! I'm really depressed, but I'm not eating over this. And that's a miracle.

> I loved a man who wasn't right for me. We'd make up and break up for weeks and finally, for my recovery and sanity, we broke up...and in one month, he got engaged and married. The girl he married gained 60 pounds. Maybe that's what it took to be in that relationship with him—but I wasn't willing to do that.

> I can't believe it. I work at pastry bar, and I don't eat the pastries. I like myself now, and I can say how I really feel and that I don't have to be perfect. I really am in recovery, and you can be too!

> My father is an alcoholic, and I always tried to please him, even to the point of the Olympics. But now, I don't do things half-assed, I do it for me...I'm not so rigid and demanding as I used to be on my boyfriend.

The second theme involves progress in the area of emotional health. A common form of encouragement to the newcomer is "Progress, not perfection." Therefore, small gains in this particular setting frequently attain heroic proportions.

I went back to work. It was rough at first. There was a jar of candy on my desk for me, and I gave it away. It's just one day at a time for me though. That's all I have to worry about. For me, a sponsor helps. I need to be guided. I call and tell her my feelings and about my day. I stay connected that way.

I used clothes, food, and alcohol and drugs. I love to spend money. I'm even a professional shopper. I love to spend anybody's money. It was all very exciting. But I never balanced my checkbook...I'd be overdrawn. So it got to be painful....I had to change everything in my life, and it's a lot better now than it ever was.

Another essential area of growth is in the realm of spiritual development. Patients are told that they are spiritually sick. "There is a part of us that has lost faith in everything, and that's why we eat." They are then informed that in order to abstain from their particular compulsions (binging, vomiting, starving), they have to keep in fit spiritual condition. Therefore, the spiritual aspect of the program is presented in the luminary sagas as a primary causal ingredient in recovery.

Before I came here, my top weight was 280 pounds. Now I weigh about 180 pounds...it's changed my life. Today I make a lot of little surrenders. I can't make it on my own...God knows better when I am ready, all I have to do is the footwork. One day at a time, ya know?

Even a year later [being recovered], there are still cravings, and I've learned not to be afraid of it. I have a program to deal with it. [Reports a returning alumna speaker during education group.]

[Staff member] This program has been a real miracle for me. Everything fell into place. Now I meditate every day. It keeps me sane.

In addition to the accolades concerning the importance of a spiritual program, accepting that one is powerless in certain situations is repeatedly stressed.

My son is an addict, and there's a lot of pain there. But I am a compulsive overeater, alcoholic, addict and vomiter. And that won't change my son. And eating won't change what I am. I accept me. I love me, and I like me today.

When I came, I felt I'd be a success if I wasn't fat and had a boyfriend. Then I got thin and married. And I said I'd be a success if I had a house...but now I see it's important to be satisfied and accepting of who and what is in my life and satisfied with the pace with which I move to rectify things. No matter what you say you want, you get what you need.

Luminary sagas follow a similar format to the other two types of stories. There is a sharing of painful events of the past, followed by a reporting of current experiences. A major distinction is that their current experience is extemely positive. These people's success stories end on a hopeful, upbeat note.

> I was married to a practicing alcoholic and compulsive overeater. We used to use together every day. And I was into my recovery for several months when I decided I wanted out—I mean out of this marriage. It would have been a big fight and struggle. But they [counselors] told me to wait a year to turn it over and see....I did. And I decided I still wanted to leave. But this time there was no fight or struggle. I accepted it, and it just happened...but I had to work my program.

There are several lessons to this story. First, a patient has to "work the program": by "admitting one is powerless," "accepting" this position, and then "taking the necessary steps of action" in areas where control is possible. An implicit assumption by the staff and patient is that she can not recover unless she "works the program" according to staff philosophy. Second, the patient must turn to counselors for guidance. Counselors are seen as people who have recovered from their eating disorders and can, therefore, share their expertise. The covert message is that the recovery program offers wisdom and guidance on more than just the physical (food-related) level. The messge is that the patient must recover on a mental or emotional and spiritual level as well. This is what is meant by the commonly used expression "turn it over." The patient has to learn that she can control certain things (like what goes into the mouth), but the rest has to be admitted and willingly "turned over" to a Higher Power.

THE LESSON

Although the lesson or moral of the story may be overt or covert, there are several underlying purposes. First, storytelling is self-reinforcing. As the storyteller continues to revise and reconstruct her biography, during the liminal and discharge stages, she incorporates an identity that explains past behavior in terms of "illness"—therefore, she is not responsible for her actions. She also receives support and encouragement from peers for assuming the identity of a "compulsive overeater."

A second function is that an obedience display toward staff ideology is successfully demonstrated through patients' use of storytelling. When a patient appropriately incorporates the necessary elements of "painful past experiences" and "current remarkable success" due to her "personality transformation" in her story, she corroborates the SED philosophy and practices.

In addition, the storyteller shares in order that the listener might gain some insight into her own life; her moral career in SED. For example, there is an implied message in many tormented tales that the family is sicker that the compulsive over/undereater, and that the family is involved in a complex power struggle. The listeners are reminded of this so that they can "correctly" assess the family dynamics and their own "disease" according to the clinic's ideology.

There is a corollary message that the family is ultimately "not responsible for your life—you are." This message is usually sent through luminary sagas with variations to the theme that each individual's own needs are paramount. "Have to see what's in the way of getting your needs met," remarked a staff member to a patient concerning her story. Along with the necessity of discovering and confronting the true self, another lesson is that of pragmatically addressing the problem. "It's not the mountains you stumble over, it's the molehills."

While the above messages stress self-responsibility, messages are often conflicting. They also have a deterministic or spiritual flavor. Sayings such as, "God knows better when I am ready" or "No matter what you say you want, please [God] let me want what I have" are encouraged by the clinical staff. These patients hold a common message of "surrender" and "acceptance" for the storyteller and her audience. And these statements support Myerhoff's (1978) proposal that through storytelling the individual represents the cultural identity of the group:

> When sacred symbols are employed in rituals, when the poles fuse, a single experiential reality is created and the individual becomes the embodiment of certain of the collectivities' beliefs (p. 257).

In addition to attempting to repair what Goffman (1963) describes as a "spoiled identity," luminary sagas also present many opportunities for positive sanctioning. In other words, storytelling provides socially sanctioned ways for individuals to encourage institutionally approved behavior. As one counselor told an aftercare patient in preparation for her final normalization ceremony "I'd like you to work on your perfectionism. You know how important it is to you. I want you to pitch about it at a couple of meetings. You really are grounded in failure—so I want you to give your success story talk. A real success story pitch!" However, the most common forms of social sanctioning are variations of the following encouraging statement from a counselor to a patient: "I feel closer to you because you shared your story...you look (softer, happier, more serene, stronger, more determined) than I've ever seen you."

Overall, storytelling is an important mechanism for maintaining stability on SED. It is used to inculcate the customs, values, and rules in the newcomer and the unengaged, to reward conformity, to punish deviation, to provide rationalizations when rituals and traditions are challenged, to instill contentment with the status quo on the unit, and to provide emotional escape from the injustices of life. Storytelling maintains the institution and forces patients into conformity. Paradoxically, it is simultaneously a socially approved outlet for the repression imposed by these same institutions.

Stories express the morals or ethics of the group. They are convenient standards for appraising behavior in terms of the approved norms. Because they are often dramatic or satirical presentations, they are an ideal method for commenting on the behavior of the storyteller and others. Stories express social approval and disapproval; praise for those who conform to accepted social mores and criticism of those who deviate. Consistent emphasis is on the conformity to the "recovery" program, to the social mores and to the ideal forms of behavior. Stories also smooth the general dissatisfaction with an individual's slow rate of progress. Stories are used to adjust new patients to the clinical setting and to convince them to accept their "disease." They warn the dissatisfied or the over-ambitious individual to be content with her lot, to accept the world as it is and her place in it and, thus, to conform to the accepted patterns. Thus, there is conformity in terms of the types of stories shared as well as when and where sharing is appropriate.

In conclusion, storytelling provides a unique source of information about the people who work and live on the eating disorder unit. It can furnish answers to questions that, if asked directly, will probably not be answered. Storytelling is effective partially because people are not completely aware of this function. It is often undervalued and underestimated by those who, although they enjoy it, do not necessarily consider that telling stories to an inquiring sociologist is unethical. In fact, when I presented my outline for a paper on storytelling to the clinical director, her response was one of incredulous boredom. "Oh, you really want to do *that*?" In other words, people do not realize how much of themselves they are giving away when they allow a researcher to collect their tales, stories, and sagas.

In fact, storytelling provides information on a variety of levels for the researcher. It gives leads for the investigation of the content of the cultural milieu (Langness and Frank 1985); it provides a nonethnocentric approach to the ways of life of a particular group, emphasizing the things that are important in their own minds (Myerhoff 1978); it offers clues to past events and rituals; it may provide a means of obtaining information on esoteric features and it reveals the affective elements such as attitudes, values, and goals (Bascom 1954). One brilliant example of an autobiographer's skill in analyzing story content is Barbara Myerhoff's 1978 commentary on a community of elderly Jews in Venice, California. She says that her subjects sought validity and meaning for their lives. In her study of the elderly,

> ...the created personal myths...truth and completeness of accounts were never at issue in this work, and no one questioned private or shared pasts. As people brought in dreams, wishes, and questions about ultimate concerns, often profanely interlarded with daily, trivial matters, woven into the always pungent, swift, funny cutting interchanges among them (Meyerhoff 1978, p. 37).

Out of memories and experiences Myerhoff, like myself, sought to discover the "human experience." However, I also demonstrate how under certain circumstances, individuals' interpretation of themselves can be reconstructed, calling into question the initial conclusions and views one holds about one's identity and behavior.

Chapter VII

Conclusion

This ethnography focuses on the basic processes of social control in an eating disorders clinic and highlights the relationships among various mechanisms by which staff control clients. Social control is linked to such mechanisms as labeling and emotion management through a process of liminality, wherein the patients are "betwixt and between" social roles and statuses. The staff assign patients to nonentity positions to make them more vulnerable and receptive to staff philosophy and practices.

These women patients have perceived and affirmatively responded to the societal expectation that they must hospitalize themselves in order to undergo a transformation to a more "normal" condition. In order for patients to recover from their "disease" of "compulsive overeating," staff believes patients have to undergo an extensive psychological and spiritual transformation. During this liminal phase of "getting better," patients are stripped of their old identity, given a new ("spoiled") identity and trained to display appropriate emotions as a means of controlling their dysfunctional eating. Patients receive various labels and participate in universal and specialized rituals of reformation designed by staff as a means of social control.

Staff assign three levels of deviance designations throughout the moral career of these patients. The first, DSM-III, is related to the political economy of medical treatment and the American insurance industry. The second label refers to the universal patient and the co-addicted family members and is associated with the current medical-model and the American self-help movement. And, finally, the third or onward types of labeling are connected to the everyday life on the SED unit. Each of these levels of labeling are linked together by the underlying assumption that these women patients are deviant because they violate a norm governing physical appearance and/or eating behavior.

Turner (1967) proposes that the neophyte in a state of liminality must absorb the knowledge and wisdom of the group, which is usually representative of the traditional cultural values and norms of the larger community, in order to attain the new status. On SED, the patients prepare for the reaggregation to a "recovered" status by assimilating the norms, standards and values set forth on SED by staff and by displaying appropriate behaviors and emotions.

For example, staff believe that when a patient is expressing her angry feelings by compulsively overeating, she is "sick." The effects of overeating, such as unwanted weight gain, lower self-esteem, increased withdrawal and social isolation, are ascribed by the clinic staff as a "sick" way of handling emotions. Therefore, proper emotion management is seen as the most effective means of controlling eating behavior.

While the staff and patients perceive hospitalization as necessary for "recovering," at the point of discharge, the overwhelming majority of patients are also convinced that the process is personally beneficial despite, for many, unremarkable weight loss results. However, there is an insidious effect that the multiplicity of stigmatizations has on the self-esteem and identity of these patients. It is evident from the storytelling responses of patients that they incorporate, during the liminal phase of hospitalization, the attributes of an eternally "spoiled identity" of which there is no hope for cure or eventual "normalization" of identity.

This research amplifies several areas of the sociological literature. It contributes to labeling theory by demonstrating a more complex framework of how labels work and challenges the concept of only one "master status" of a deviance designation. In addition, it presents an analysis of how the labels affect the reconstruction of the self.

This work expands the literature on liminality by connecting the labels to group rituals and other processes of stripping the self and reconstituting the self throughout the liminal process. This study also adds to the literature on identity and emotion management by illustrating via ethnographic citations the various strategies staff and patients incorporate to reconstruct an "appropriate, recovering" autobiography.

Finally, of the many different perspectives on the phenomenon of eating disorders, this ethnography shows the powerful effects on everyday life of one given social construction, and how it is affected by the staff, the clinic and various moral entrepreneurs within American society.

In this particular instance, the SED appears to operate on the premise that emotional/psychological factors are the primary cause of eating disorders as opposed to the purely biological or social viewpoint proposed by other researchers and clinicians in the same field. Overall, the clinic follows a psychologically oriented medical perspective, although the staff periodically would obliquely acknowledge cultural and/or environmental influences. The staff unanimously espouse the doctrine that eating disorders are of intrapsychic origin and of such magnitude that the individual sufferer requires intensive medical intervention.

Concerning the contemporary development of eating disorders in American society, my personal bias follows the social/cultural school of thought. I, too, believe that most forms of dysfunctional eating have to do with an individual trying to take care of herself while simultaneously rebelling against stringent cultural dictates. Eating is not simply an issue of consuming appropriate amounts of nutrients. Eating is imbued with myriad values and meanings. Therefore, one of the reasons this program might be effective is because it permits patients to explore their private meanings for dysfunctional eating that perhaps will not (or even can not) be addressed in another context.

And although many problems (such as a "spoiled identity") appear to be created by the clinic, the basic premise that underlies the clinic philosophy may be legitimate. Eating appears to be related to emotions for these patients and the way in which these patients relate to eating has to do with various issues of emotion.

I had mixed personal reactions throughout my entire internship on SED. I believe, in general, that the principles espoused by Overeaters Anonymous have some positive benefit for the patients. Although I do not necessarily agree with the staff manner and means of confrontation, these initially disconsolate patients do appear more hopeful and enthusiastic at discharge.

I was most disenchanted by what I perceived as staff's inhumane treatment toward the patients in terms of labeling and some of the rituals of reformation. I was frustrated by the hypocrisy of labeling everyone "depressives" and "compulsive overeaters" despite physical and emotional differences. Initially perplexed by the private unofficial labeling by the staff, over time I became infuriated by this brutal and sadistic practice and the apparently extreme prejudicial contempt of certain staff toward a number of the patients. It required a great deal of what Hochschild (1983) refers to as "surface acting" in order for me to keep my mouth shut and play the part of a submissive intern.

There are a profusion of paradoxes regarding the phenomenon of eating disorders which range from the macro-political arena to the micro-interaction level on SED. Feminist scholars, such as Orbach (1986, p. 191), proclaim that

> Women's eating problems of all kinds arise out of the individual's attempt both to conform to and repudiate the current aesthetic idealization of women.

Therefore, the first paradox is how a private problem, such as a woman's suffering around issues of food and body size, is transformed into a collective issue that requires societal intervention.

Eating has become medicalized for the economic and political benefit of those entrepreneurs seeking profit and control. For example, Emmett (1985, p. vii) declares:

> The incidence of eating disorders is reaching epidemic proportions....In one or perhaps two decades, anorexia and bulimia have undergone a remarkable metamorphosis—from psychiatric curiosities to publicly recognized mental health emergencies.

Although Emmett proposes that eating disorders are increasingly prevalent, he also acknowledges "In the absence of a reliable means for recovery, the cost of treatment is extraordinarily expensive" (1985, p. vii).

The statement points to a variety of inconsistencies in the operation of the clinic. One is that weight loss is not a criterion of success for the hospital administration and staff, although it is extremely important to the overweight patient. This issue is apparently not a staff criterion because weight loss is so tenuous.

Another problem on the unit concerns the cost of treatment. It seems ludicrous that this is considered *medical* treatment and that insurance companies are reimbursing the hospital for very expensive in-patient care that is primarily given by paraprofessionals (with no credentials, licenses, or professional degrees) who are hired to perform the majority of the therapeutic treatment on SED.

And, finally, one more paradox concerning the treatment cost is the rather curious phenomenon of patients being discharged as "better" as soon as the policy limits are reached on their medical insurance.

Ironically, while nationally reported success rates are minimal and treatment costs prohibitive, many members of the American medical profession have an intensely cynical attitude toward such patients. Beller (1977) observes that eating disorder patients are likely to be discredited by medical staff. And in particular, she notes that obesity is given a very negative designation by the very medical community that professes the necessity of treatment. Beller (1977, p. 5) further states:

> The official orthodoxy [of practicing physicians] that fat is suicidal:
> a sin, that is, at best; and at worst a sort of felony.

Amid this social context of blaming the victim, eating disorder clinics developed as a means of controlling women's appearance and eating behavior. And what appears to be an even greater paradox is that while SED staff members claim to be "fellow sufferers" (all have gone through the program of Overeaters Anonymous) and are potentially discreditable by societal standards—several of these same staff members appear to even more harshly judge and disdainfully scorn the patients, (who are also afflicted with the disease of compulsive overeating), than does the medical community.

In support of this observation, Erving Goffman (1963, p. 37) notes that the stigmatized individual is likely to experience strong ambivalence towards his/her fellow sufferers:

> for those others will not only be patently stigmatized, and thus not
> like the normal person he knows himself to be, but may also have
> other attributes with which he finds it difficult to associate himself.

Furthermore, Goffman speculates that as a result of this ambivalence toward fellow-sufferers the stigmatized may oscillate "in his support of, identification with, and participation among his own" (p. 38).

There are additional inconsistencies concerning treatment issues. There is the paradox of a medical system that has a predominant religious component. Even though patients are hospitalized for medical treatment, in the philosophy of SED they require assistance from a "Higher Power" in order to have a "spiritual awakening" which causes the personality transformation necessary for recovery from compulsive overeating. On SED, there is a strong moral dimension to the treatment program which has to do with a sense of self and private identity.

Another treatment incongruity is the paradox of abuse in the midst of cure. There are rituals of reformation, labeling and other processes of stripping the self that appear to be a very harsh and painful means of "getting better" on this unit. Patients are also infantalized by staff and told they have "no control" during the entire liminal/social control process. Ironically, these same punitive rituals and labels are used by staff in order to teach the patients how to be *in control* of their emotions and eating behavior.

The final incongruity is the double paradox of the SED treatment program: the "cure" makes the patients "sick"—and as a result, the patients feel "better." In order to be perceived by staff as recovering from their disease, the patients paradoxically need to accept and embrace the permanently "spoiled identity" of "compulsive overeater" from which they can never be cured or have a "normal" identity. However, due to the emotionalism of the ceremonial process, these patients leave the hospital feeling "better." They accept the staff philosophy that "you are not cured, but you are well enough to go" and at discharge the majority do appear happy and (at least temporarily) free of their obsession with food.

Until the socially constructed notions of women's size and shape are expanded from their current narrow definitions of what is culturally appropriate, women will likely continue to have body-image problems. And as long as women emulate the unrealistic aesthetic standards presented by the media, they will remain trapped by the idealization of women's bodies. The media and various industries thus continue to manipulate these aesthetics—and values—and reinforce the medical-corporate pursuit of control and profit.

Eating disorders are a historically specific "social construction" and a form of "hegemonic disclosure" developed by those in power and employed as a means of social control. The perceived deviances of eating and body size are therefore subject to conscious efforts at change. Which particular female form is currently considered socially deviant or not "normal" according to societal standards exists because of the social power of those doing the deviance-defining (Schur 1984).

Stigma is not inherent in behavior or appearance. It is an emotional response that is socially generated. Stigma is a social condition that is learned, and therefore it can be unlearned. Rejection of unhealthy, rigid standards and repudiation of constraining female role definitions represent one means of helping women to surmount devaluation. SED represents another. Which approach do we as women, as a society, wish to support?.

Notes

1.   All of the names and some of the biographical characteristics are changed. Any coincidence of names I use in this ethnography with those of actual corporations, hospitals, or individuals is completely accidental. Also, I only observed one hospital ward and therefore some of the features may be idisyncratic to this one institution.

2.   This last rule was in the process of being revoked toward the end of my internship. There was such a great deal of ongoing patient protest concerning telephone policies that a change in administrative procedure concerning patient's right to privacy on the telephone occurred.

References

Allon, N. 1976. "Tensions in Interactions of Overweight Adolescent Girls." *Women and Health* 1 (2): 14-15, 18-23.

_____. 1984. "It Takes a Fatty to Know a Fatty: The Group Dieting Healing System." Paper presented to the Society of Applied Anthropology, 1971, as reported in Sobal, J. "Group dieting, the stigma of obesity, and overweight adolescents: Contributions of Natalie Allon to the sociology of obesity." In Kallen D. and Sussman M. (Eds.) *Obesity and the Family*. New York: Hathaway Press, 9-20.

American Psychiatric Association. Diagnostic and Statistical Manual of Mental Disorders, Third Edition, Revised. Washington, DC, American Psychiatric Association, 1987.

Ayers, W. M. 1958. "Changing Attitudes Toward Overweight and Reducing." *Journal of the American Dietetic Association* 34: 23-29.

Bascom, W. R. 1954. "Four Functions of Folklore," *Journal of American Folklore* 67: 333-349.

Becker, H. S. 1963. *Outsiders: Studies in the Sociology of Deviance*. New York: Free Press.

Beesom, P.B., and W. McDermott. 1979. *Textbook of Medicine*. 14th ed. City, State: Publisher.

Bell, R. M. 1985. *Holy Anorexia*. Chicago: University of Chicago Press.

Beller, A. S. 1977. *Fat and Thin: A Natural History of Obesity*. New Yourk: Farrar, Straus and Giroux.

Bender, M. 1967. The Beautiful People. New York: Coward-McCann.

Bennett, W., and J. Gurin 1982. *The Dieter's Dilemma*. New York: Basic Books.

Boskind-White, M. 1985. "Bulimarexia: A Sociocultural Perspective." In *Theory and Treatment of Anorexia Nervosa and Bulimia,* edited by S. W. Emmett, New York: Brunner/ Mazel.

Boskind-White, M., and W. White 1983. *Bulimarexia: The Binge/ Purge Cycle.* New York: W. W. Norton.

Bray, G. A. ed. 1979. Obesity in America. N.I.H. Publication No. 79-359. Washington, D.C.: U.S. Department of Health, Education, and Welfare. National Institute of Health.

Brody, J. E. 1981. "An Eating Disorder of Binges and Purges Reported Widespead." *The New York Times* (October 20), p. Cl.

Brownell, K. D. 1983a. "Obesity: Understanding and Treating a Serious, Prevalent, and Refractory Disorder." *Journal of Consulting and Clinical Psychology,* 50: 820-840.

Brownell, K. D. 1983b. "Obesity: Behavioral Treatments for a Serious Prevalent, and Refractory Problem." In *Eating and Weight Disorders,* edited by R. K. Goodstein. New York: Springer.

Bruch, H. 1973. *Eating Disorders: Obesity, Anorexia Nervosa, and the Person Within.* New York: Basic Books.

Chernin, K. 1981. *The Obsession: Reflection on the Tyranny of Slenderness.* New York: Harper and Row.

Chernin, K. 1985. *The Hungry Self.* New York: Times Books.

Conrad, P., and J. W. Schneider. 1980. *Deviance and Medicalization: From Badnes to Sickness.* St. Louis, MO: C. V. Mosby.

Douvan E., and J. Adelson. 1966. *The Adolescent Experience.* New York: Wiley.

Dundes, A. 1971. *The Study of Folklore.* Englewood Cliffs, NJ: Prentice-Hall.

Emerson, R. M., E. Rocheford, and L. Shaw. 1983. "The Micropolitics of Trouble in a Psychiatric Board and Care Facility." *Urban Life 12(3): 349-367.*

Emmet, S. W. 1985. *Theory and Treatment of Anorexia Nervosa and Bulimia. New York: Brunner/Mazel.*

Erikson, K. T. 1962. "Notes on the Sociology of Deviance." Social Problems 9:307-314.

Fairburn, C. G. 1984. "Bulimia: Its epidemiology and Management." Pp. 235-256 in *Eating and Its Disorders,* edited by A. J. Stunkard and E. Stellan. New York: Raven Press.

Ferraro K. J. 1983. "Negotiating Trouble in a Battered Women's Shelter." *Urban Life,* 12(3): 287-306.

Fiedler, L. A. 1960. "Good Good Girls and Good Bad Boys: Clarissa As a Juvenile." Pp. 254-272 in *Love and Death in The American Novel.* New York: Criterion.

For Today. 1982. Torrance, CA: Overeaters Anonymous.

Ford, C. S., and F. A. Beach. 1951. *Patterns of Sexual Behavior.* New York: Harper & Row.

Friedman, A. 1974. *Fat Can Be Beautiful: Stop Dieting, Start Living. New York: Berkley.*

Garb, J. L., J. R. Garb, and A. J. Stunkard. 1975. "Social Factors and Obesity in Navaho Indian Children." Pp. 37-39 in Recent Advances in Obesity Research I, edited by A. Howard. London: Newman

Garland, M. 1960. *The Changing Face of Beauty.* London: Weidenfield and Nicholson.

Garland, M. 1970. *The Changing Forum of Fashion.* New York: Praeger.

Garn, S. M. 1983. "Some Consequences of Being Obese." In *Controversies in Obesity,* edited by B. Hansen. New York: Praeger.

Garn, S. M., S. M. Bailey, and P. E. Cole. 1980. "Continuities and Changes in Fatness and Obesity." In *Nutrition, Physiology and Obesity, edited by R. Schemmel. Palm Beach, FL: Raven Press.*

Garn, S. M., S. M. Bailey, P. E. Cole and I. Higgins. 1977. "Level of Education, Level of Income and Level of Fatness in Adults." American Journal of Clinical Nutrition, 30: 721-725.

Garn, S. M., S. M. Bailey, and I. Higgins. 1980. 'Effects of Socioeconomic Status, Family Line and Living-Together on Fatness and Obesity." In *Childhood Prevention of Athersclerosis and Hypertension,* edited by R. Lauer and R. Shekelle. New York: Raven Press

Garn, S. M., and D. C. Clark. 1976. "Family-line Origins of Obesity." In *Second Wyeth Nutrition Symposium,* edited by L. A. Barness. New York: Wyeth Laboratories.

Garn, S. M., M. LaVelle, and P. J. Hopkins. 1983. "Fatness Correlations of Parents and Children Living Together and Living Apart." *American Journal of Clinical Nutrition.*

Garn, S. M., M. LaVelle, and J. J. Pilkington. 1984. "Obesity and Living Together." Pp. 33-47 in *Obesity and the Family,* edited by D. Kallen and M. Sussman. New York: Haworth Press.

Gilligan, C. 1982. *In a Different Voice: Psychological Theory and Women's Development.* Cambridge: Harvard University Press.

Goffman, E. 1963. *Stigma: Notes on the Management of Spoiled Identity.* Englewood Cliffs NJ: Prentice Hall.

Goffman, E. 1961. *Asylums: Essays on the Social Situation of Mental Patients and Other Inmates.* Garden City, NJ: Anchor Books.

Goldblatt, P. B., M. E. Moore, and A. J. Stunkard. 1973. "Social Factors in Obesity." In *The Psychology of Obesity,* edited by N. Krell. Springfield, IL: Charles C. Thomas

Gordon, J. B., and A. Tobias. 1984. "Fat, Female and the Life Course: The Developmental Years." Pp. 65-92 in *Obesity and the Family,* edited by D. J. Kallen and M. B. Sussman. New York: Haworth Press

Gubrium, J. F., and D. R. Buckholdt. 1982. *Describing Care: Image and Practice in Rehabilitation.* Boston, MA: Oelgeschlager, Gunn, and Hain.

Halmi, K.A., J. R. Falk, and E. Schwartz. 1982. "Binge-eating and vomiting: A Survey of a College Population." *Psychological Medicine II* 1: 697-706.

Hochschild, A. R. 1983. *The Managed Heart: Commercialization of Human Feeling.* Berkeley: University of California Press.

House, R. C., R. Grisius, and M. M. Bliziotes. 1981. "Perimolysis: Unveiling the Surreptitious Vomiter." *Oral Surgery,* 51: 152-155.

Hymowitz, C., and M. Weissman. 1978. *A History of Women in America.* New York: Bantam Books.

Kallen, D., and A. Doughty. 1984. "The Relationship of Weight, the Self Perception of Weight and Self Esteem with Courtship Behavior." Pp. 93-114 in *Obesity and the Family,* edited by D. Kallen and M. Sussman. New York: Haworth Press.

Keys, A. J. Brozek, A. Henschel, O. Mickelson, and H. L. Taylor. 1950. *The Biology of Human Starvation.* Minneapolis: University of Minnesota Press.

Krieshok, S. I., and a D. H. Karpowitz. 1988. "A Review of Selected Literature on Obesity and Guidelines for Treatment." *Journal of Counseling and Development* 66: 326-330.

Langness, L. L., and G. Frank. 1985. *Lives, An Anthropological Approach to Biography.* Novato, CA: Chandler and Sharp.

Laslett, B., and C. A. B. Warren. 1975. "Losing Weight: The Organizational Promotion of Behavior Change." *Social Problem* 23: 69-80.

Lemert, E. M. 1951. *Social Pathology.* New York: McGraw—Hill.

_____. 1967. *Human Deviance, Social Problems and Social Control.* Englewood Clifs, NJ: Prentice-Hall.

Mayer, J. 1968. *Overweight: Causes, Cost, and Control.* Englewood Cliffs, NJ: Prentice-Hall.

Messenger, J. C., Jr. 1959. "The Role of Proverbs in a Nigerian Judicial System." *Southwestern Journal of Anthropology,* 15: 64-73.

Millman, M. 1977. *The Unkindist Cut: Life in the Backrooms of Medicine.* New York: William Marrow and Company.

_____. 1980. *Such a Pretty Face: Being Fat in America.* New York: Norton.

Moore, M. E., A. J. Stunkard and L. Srole. 1960. "Obesity, Social Class, and Mental Illness." *Journal of the American Medical Association,* 181: 962-966.

Myerhoff, B. 1978. *Number Our Days.* New York: E. P. Dutton.

Orbach, S. 1978. *Fat is a Feminist Issues: A Self—Help Guide for Compulsive Eaters.* New York: Berkley Books.

_____. 1982. *Fat is a Feminist Issue II: A Program to Conquer Compulsive Eating.* New York: Berkley Books.

_____. 1986. *Hunger Strike.* New York: Norton.

Ort, R. S., A. B. Ford, and R. E. Liske. 1964. "The Doctor Patient Relationship As Described by Physicians and Medical Students." *Journal of Health and Human Behavior,* 5: 25-34.

Overeaters Anonymous. 1980. Torrance, CA: Overeaters Anonymous.

Palazzoli, M. S. 1967. *Self-Starvation: From Individual to Family Therapy in the Treatment of Anorexia Nervosa.* New York: Jason Aronson.

Papper, S. 1970. "The Undesirable Patient." *Journal of Chronic Diseases,* 22: 777-779.

Passin, H., and J. W. Bennett. 1943. "Changing Agricultural Magic in Southern Illinois—Systematic Analysis of Folk-Urban Transition." *Social Forces,* 22: 98-106.

Pope, H., and J. Hudson. 1985. "Biological Treatments of Eating Disorders." In *Theory and Treatment of Anorexia Nervosa and Bulimia,* edited by S. W. Emmett. New York: Brunner/Mazel.

Pyle, R. L., J. E. Mitchell, E. E. Eckert, P. A. Halvorson, P. A. Neuman, and G. M. Goff. 1983. "The Incidence of Bulimia in Freshman College Students." *The International Journal of Eating Disorders* 2: 75-85.

Rader, W. 1980. "A Disease of the Mind." Pp. 183-187 in *Overeaters Anonymous.* Torrance, CA: Overeaters Anonymous.

Ratliff, B., and J. McVoy. 1988. "Atypical Eating Disorders." In S. W. Millholland, "New Frontiers with Eating Disorders," *Family Therapy News,* 19(6): 10.

Rimm, A. A., and P. L. White. 1979. "Obesity: Its Risks and Hazards." Pp. 103-124 *Obesity in America,* edited by G. Bray. N.I.H. Publication #79-359. Washington, DC: U.S. Department of Health, Education, and Welfare. National Institute of Health.

Ross, C. E., and J. Mirowsky. 1983. "Social Epidemiology of Overweight: A Substantive and Methodological Investigation." *Journal of Health and Social Behavior,* 24: 288-298.

Rudofsky, B. 1971. *The Unfashionable Human Body.* New York: Doubleday.

Schur, E. M. 1984. *Labeling Women Deviant: Gender, Stigma and Social Control.* New York: Random House.

Schwartz, M. A. 1984. "Expansionary America Tightens its Belt: Social Scietific Perspectives on Obesity." Pp. 49-63 in *Obesity and the Family,* edited by D. J. Kallen and M. B. Sussman.

Sobal, J. 1984. "Marriage, Obesity and Dieting." Pp. 139-155 in *Obesity and the Family,* edited by D. J. Kallen and M. B. Sussman. New York: Haworth Press.

Sours, J. A. 1979. "The Primary Anorexia Nervosa Syndrome." In *Basis Handbook of Child Psychiatry, Volume II,* edited by J. D. Noshpitz. New York: Basic Books.

————. 1980. *Starving to Death in a Sea of Objects: The Anorexia Nervosa Syndrome.* New York: Jason Aronson.

Spack, N. P. 1985. "Medical Complications of Anorexia Nervosa and Bulimia." In *Theory and Treatment of Anorexia and Bulimia,* edited by S. W. Emmett. New York: Brunner/Mazel.

Stangler, R. S., and A. M. Printz. 1980. "DSM-III: Psychiatric Diagnosis in a University Population." *American Journal of Psychiatry* 137: 937-940.

Stern, M. P., J. A. Pugh, S. P. Gaskill, and H. P. Hazuda. 1982. "Knowledge, Attitudes, and Behavior Related to Obesity and Dieting in Mexican Americans and Anglos: The San Antonio Heart Study." *American Journal of Epidemiology* 115: 917-927.

Stimson, G. V. 1974. "Obeying Doctor's Orders: A View from the Other Side." *Social Science and Medicine* 8: 97-104.

Stuart, R., and B. Davis. 1972. *Slim Chance in a Fat World: Behavioral Control of Obesity*. Champaign, IL: Research Press.

Stunkard, A. 1958. "The Management of Obesity." *New York State Journal of Medicine* 58: 79-87.

_____. 1976. *The Pain of Obesity*. Palo Alto, CA: Bull Publishing Company.

Sussman, M. 1956. "Psycho-social Correlates of Obesity: Failure of Calorie Collectors." *Journal of the American Dietetic Association* 32: 327-334.

Toelken, B. 1979. *The Dynamics of Folklore*. Boston: Houghton Mifflin.

Turner, V. 1967. *The Ritual Process: Structure and Anti-Structure*. Chicago: Aldine.

The U.S. Health Examination Survey 1960-62 and Health and Nutrition Examination Survey 1971-74. 1979. National Center for Health Statistics. Weight by height and age for adults 18-74 years: United States, 1971-74. Vital and Health Statistics, Series 11, #208.

Van Gennep, A. 1960. *The Rites of Passage*. Translated by M. B. Vizedom and G. L. Caffee. London: Routledge and Kegan Paul.

Vander Zanden, J. W. 1979. *Sociology*. New York: Wiley.

Wang, B. 1935. "Folksongs as Regulators of Politics." *Sociology and Social Research* 20: 161-166.

Warren, C. A. B. 1983. "The Politics of Trouble in an Asolescent Psychiatric Hospital." *Urban Life* 12(3): 327-348.

Warren, M. P. and R. L. Van de Wiele. 1973. "Clinical and Metabolic Features of Anorexia Nervosa." *American Journal of Obstetrics and Gynecology 117: 435-449.*

Weil, W. B. 1984. "Demographic Determinants of Obesity." Pp. 21-32 in Obesity and the-Family, edited by D. Kallen and M. Sussman. New York: Haworth Press.

West, K. M. 1974. "Culture, History and Adiposity, or Should Santa Claus Reduce? *Obesity and Bariatric Medicine* 2(2): 48-52.

Woodman, M. 1980. *The Owl Was a Baker's Daughter: Obesity, Anorexia Nervosa and the Repressed Feminine.* Toronto, Canada: Inner City Books.